INTERCESSORS
ARiSE

&

Finding your Authority

by

Sandy Warner

Intercessors Arise & Finding Our Authority

Visions, Dreams, Still Small Voice, Testimonies, Quotes, Prophetic
Words, Stories, Articles, Word Studies
Compiled by Sandy Warner

Published by: SOS Publications®
PO Box 7096 • Eugene, Oregon 97401

ISBN 978-0-6152-1516-7
Copyright © 2008 by Sandy Warner.
Printed in the United States of America.
First printing 1999, 80 pages.
Second Edition 2008, 220 pages

To contact author: swauthor@usa.net
WEBSITE: www.thequickenedword.com

TABLE OF CONTENTS

PART ONE: IDENTIFYING INTERCESSORS 6
   Intercessors Arise! 6
   The Characteristics Of An Intercessor 11
   8 Pillars Of A Living Intercessor 15
   Intercessors Are Peace Makers 20
   Intercessors Are Like Barometers 24
   Intercessors Express Godly Longings 41
   The Heart Of Prayer 45

PART TWO: TYPES OF INTERCESSIONS 46
Intercession Is Repentance 46
   What To Do About Judgment 46
   How To Restore Church Power 47
   Godly Sorrow Produces Repentance/ Change ... 51
   After The Call (On 7/07/07) 53

Intercession Is Forgiveness 54
   What Is Forgiveness 54
   To Forgive 64

Intercession Is A Sacrifice Of Standing In The Gap ... 65
   To Take The Heat 66
   Keeping The Children 69
   Parents Abiding Keeps Your Progeny 72
   To Partner With Him In Prayer 74
   Holding Onto Your Loved Ones 76
   Rescue Our Prodigals 82
   To Stand For A Friend 82
   Standing In The Gap For Our Troops 85
   Standing In The Breach Of The "Fault" Line 86
   Bible Study Of Isaiah 58 - God's Chosen Fast 89

How To Intercede 92
   How To Battle Safely 92
   How To Occupy 94
   To Partner With Him In Prayer 101

How To Watch And Pray 103
Simple Prayer, Resting Faith 106
Praying Out Loud Or Silent? 112
Prayer Through Poetry 114
Teach Me To Pray 115
Intercession Is Importunity 116
Persistence In Prayer Opens Doors 119
Persistence, Don't Give Up 123

The Burden Of Prayer 126
Bear One Another's Burdens 126
Groaning Over The Orphans 129
Tears Are Prayers 131
Tears Opening The Heavens 132

Tongues In Prayer 134
Tongues And The Porthole 134
Tongues: Awesome Corporate Authority 136

PART THREE: AUTHORITY OF INTERCESSOR 136
Finding Your Metron 136
The Power Of His Word 142
What Will You Decree? 144
Stand Boldly And Declare His Word 147
Intercessors Battle Strongholds In Mindsets ... 148
Restoring The Doorkeeper 152
Inheritance Of Ruling And Reigning 161
Authority Over Weather 163
Use Your Authority Over Creation 166
Angels And Warfare 168
The Wall, The Angels And Revival 172

PART FOUR: WARNINGS TO INTERCESSORS 176
Soul Power And Head Knowledge 176
Soul Power Vs Thy Kingdom Come 178
How To Close The Doors To Backlash 180
Follow Your Conscience: Divine Restraints 187

PART FIVE: EXAMPLES OF INTERCESSIONS 190
Bob Jones Importance Of Prayer 190

Prayer Meeting: Free The Desperate..................192
Prayer Meeting: The Breaker Anointing..............193
Prayer Meeting: Breaking Strongholds 198
United Intercessors: An Arrow In The Sky 200
Intercession For the Davids And Michals..........201
Prayer & Supernatural Deliverance.....................204
Intercession Over Grieving The Holy Spirit......204
Prayer On October 31 214
Prayer On Sundown Yom Kipper........................215

PART ONE:
IDENTIFYING INTERCESSORS

INTERCESSORS ARISE!

BOB JONES VISION:
www.bobjones.org

Bob was sitting with some other folk at a table eating. The Lord came to the table and Bob thought 'Oh good, He has come to eat with us', but Jesus said, 'I have not come to eat with you now, I have come to ask you to pray with Me, I am raising up the school of intercession.' Bob said this is the time when the Lord is anointing intercessors and inviting them to pray with Him, out of a spirit of revelation." {end quote}

The following is a vision of hope, whereby the Lord is restoring intercession. If you do not consider yourself an intercessor, please consider the possibility as you read the following vision. There are people worldwide, whose callings are hidden even to themselves, and the Lord is wanting to restore their position in Him. He is trumpeting a timely and an urgent call to prayer, and it is happening right now.

Vision given to Jeff Ching 3/25/99
(Mercy Seat Church in Lynnwood, WA.)
worldflair@yahoo.com

Part I
I saw a very large mass of intercessors stuck in what I was impressed to be miry clay. I saw different people struggling with this miry clay, most were engulfed up to their hips and some up to their arms. I noticed that they struggled in vain

6

not being able to free themselves. Along the banks I saw many people yelling and they were stretching out sticks and boards and some throwing ropes to help pull out the intercessors. The intercessors reached out to those that were trying to help them but none were being pulled out. I became aware of another large group of intercessors at the right hand of God in Christ. They were interceding to God on behalf of the intercessors stuck in the miry clay. Suddenly I saw the hands of all the entrapped intercessors being lifted heavenward accompanied with great praise and worship from their mouths. Through great open heavens the hand and arm of God reached down and pulled out the intercessors stuck in the miry clay.

Ps 40:2 He brought me up also out of an horrible pit, out of the miry clay, and set my feet upon a rock, and established my goings. (KJV)

Part II
There was before me a very vast forest. In this forest I saw multitudes of intercessors. All in this forest were lost and wandering around not seeming to have direction or purpose. At times a few would meet by accident and pray but because the forest was so thick with brush and blackberry bushes over a persons head they soon lost each other. Most were wandering trying to find a way out of this vast forest. There was a semi-darkness caused by the huge trees that grew everywhere. Things seemed so confused, I had a lost feeling.

Then suddenly there was an extremely bright light that appeared at a distance. I saw all the intercessors in this vast forest turn and head toward that light as if urged or compelled by some great force. At first it was very difficult for them because of the thick underbrush. They beat paths with large sticks through this brush as they made their ways toward this light. As they got closer they found it easier and easier as others closer to this light had made paths for them all heading in the same direction. Soon I looked and started to see at first a few people, and then many on paths all heading toward this great light. An excitement could be sensed in the air. All of these small paths started to join into larger paths until at the edge of the forest their was one large path filled with intercessors praising and worshipping God.

Prov 4:18 But the path of the just is as the shining light, that shineth more and more unto the perfect day. (KJV)

Part III
The next scene was a desert place with sand dunes, and at some places, large rocks. There was little to no plant or animal life. It was a very hot and dry desert. As I looked upon this desert there again were God's intercessors. They were all prostrated in the desert sands. Very little movement came from them and as God showed me a closer look I saw that they were all dying with many near death. Vultures hovered and swooped down on many of these intercessors trying to pluck out their eyes and hearts. It had appeared by their tracks that many had wandered for sometime searching for water and food but could not find any.

They were scattered all over this desert with small groups here and there but mostly individuals separated for some reason or another. I saw a few lift their head, stand up and walk toward what seemed to be an oasis. At first it seemed to be an illusion of some sort that often accompanies such desperate situations. Maybe angel messengers from God? Suddenly, I was standing in the midst of this oasis which was not very large, nor ornately beautiful. It was just an oasis with a few trees and a pond of water. As I looked toward the sand dunes in the distance, I saw a figure of a person rise forth silhouetted against the sky coming toward this oasis. Then looking in other directions a few more. These few soon arrived at the oasis and quickly refreshed themselves and immediately started to praise and worship God.

They started to intercede for others they had met in the desert and soon afterwards more and more started to arrive. Soon the oasis was overcrowded with vast numbers of people. I then realized that the oasis had started to expand and expand and expand. The desert was turning into a beautiful oasis farther than the eye could see. I could see no end to the expansion of the oasis. The oasis had expanded to encompass the intercessors.

Isa 35:1-8 The wilderness and the solitary place shall be glad for them; and the desert shall rejoice, and blossom as the rose. It shall blossom abundantly, and rejoice even with joy and singing: the glory of Lebanon shall be given unto it, the excellency of Carmel and Sharon, they shall see the glory of the LORD, and the excellency of our God. Strengthen ye the weak hands, and confirm the feeble knees. Say to them that are of a fearful heart, Be strong, fear not: behold, your God will come with vengeance, even God with a recompence; he will come and save you. Then the eyes of the blind shall be opened, and the ears of the deaf shall be unstopped. Then shall the lame man leap as an hart, and the tongue of the dumb sing: for in the wilderness shall waters break out, and streams in the desert. And the parched ground shall become a pool, and the thirsty land springs of water: in the habitation of dragons, where each lay, shall be grass with reeds and rushes. And an highway shall be there, and a way, and it shall be called The way of holiness; the unclean shall not pass over it; but it shall be for those: the wayfaring men, though fools, shall not err therin. (KJV)

{end quote From Jeff Ching}

WORD TO PONDER: FOR SUCH A TIME AS THIS 1997

Behind closed doors I prepared you. I carefully allotted you hidden assignments, ones that would build courage and valor. — Assignments that built faith against the odds. I raised you to be gracious in your manner and I gave you My greatest favor. Even so, who would have guessed that in your veins flows the blood of royalty? Who would have guessed I would have chosen you for such an hour? For behind closed doors, you were anointed. Behind closed doors, you were prepared. In secret, I raised an intercessor, a deliverer. The measure of your authority, your vote, has been kept secret even from you.

The enemy has secretly plotted to kill and destroy and annihilate. I have exposed his plans just in time that you may take your rightful place. Rise to the occasion, queen daughter. For I have given you the anointing of Queen Esther. Come forth My beloved and speak to the King. I have given you the power and the authority to intercede on behalf of the many who can not speak for themselves. I have strategically placed you in My kingdom for such a time as this. Have courage, speak forth My Words. Be strong, be valiant and fight for those who can not fight. Be My deliverer and put a stop to this enemy plan.

I stretch out My scepter to you. Step forward into your place. What is your request? I will give it to you. Speak and hold nothing back. What is your petition My queen?

"Then Esther the queen answered and said, If I have found favour in thy sight, O king, and if it please the king, let my life be given me at my petition, and my people at my request: 4 For we are sold, I and my people, to be destroyed, to be slain, and to perish. But if we had been sold for bondmen and bondwomen, I had held my tongue, although the enemy could not countervail the king's damage." (Esther 7:3-4)

WORD TO PONDER: FIGHT AND PRAY FOR YOUR COUNTRY 9/16/00

Intercessors arise and knock upon My door. Call upon My Name, and unsheathe your swords. Force back the deeds of darkness. And I will be with you even in times of darkness over your nation. I will never leave you. Fight and pray for your country, for I desire My light to shine and bring in a new day. I want to fill My house with My glory. Pray My Word and My promises. Declare them over your cities, over your countries, over your nations. And see that I will arise to answer your call.

"The king proclaims the LORD's decree: "The LORD said to me, `You are my son.

Today I have become your Father. Only ask, and I will give you the nations as your inheritance, the ends of the earth as your possession." (Ps 2:7-8 NLT)

THE CHARACTERISTICS OF AN INTERCESSOR

An intercessor is a person who by calling or by nature chooses to be a mediator on behalf of those who cannot intervene for themselves. Intercessors make requests, urge, plead, beg, counsel, discuss, risk, sacrifice, and make war on issues relating to the weaker ones, and thus they have an impact on the final outcomes for those they serve.

There is a difference between a person who is called an intercessor and a person who prays. Any person can pray, but not all praying people are intercessors. The opposite is true also - an intercessor may live his entire life and live to make only one great act of intercession. The differences of an intercessor are subtle - hidden in the life and heart behind the prayer. There are many examples of intercessors in the Bible, and they walked with the favor to impact and change God's heart. Consider the following role models and their characteristics:

~ THE FUNCTIONS OF AN INTERCESSOR ~
1. TO RISK & SACRIFICE
1) Moses was willing to be blotted out of God's book. (Ex 32:32)
2) Abraham was willing to suffer God's possible displeasure by negotiating Him down to 10 godly men in Sodom & Gomorrah. (Genesis 18:22)
3) When king David disobeyed by taking a census, he was willing to be destroyed in order to seek safety for his people. (1 Chron 21:17)
4) Daniel was willing to talk with God when He was very angry. (Dan 9:16)
5) Jesus was willing to become sin and lay down His life so that others could find forgiveness. (Isa 53:12)
6) The Centurion was willing to approach authority as well as subject himself to it. (Matt 8:5)
7) Martha dared to risk her friendship with Jesus to challenge His decision of delay. (John 11:21-22)
8) A father risked public exposure, fear of man's opinions, and disappointment for the sake of interceding for his possessed son. (Mark 9:17)
9) The Nobleman risked his self-sufficient pride. He could not help his son but he knew who could. He also risked public exposure and reputation. (John 4:49)
10) Stephen was willing to face the murderous rage of a crowd and asked God to forgive them. (Acts 7:59)
11) Esther was willing to perish at risk of defending her people to the king. At the very least she was willing to face a life of ill-favor, isolation and banishment from the king's court. (Esther 4:16)
12) David as a young boy was willing to face death from Goliath for the sake of Israel. At the very least he was willing to face humiliation, failure and defeat. (1 Sam 17:37)

2. TO BOLDLY DEFEND

Each of the above role models defended with boldness. This does not necessarily mean they had naturally bold personalities. Watch a mother or father bird when a threat comes too close to their nest! God has placed within His creation an instinct to defend the young. An intercessor's heart comes to the surface when they perceive a threat. Suddenly the heart of a pussy cat turns into the roar of a lion. (Heb 4:16)

3. TO VOLUNTEER
One of the marks of an intercessor is a willingness to do something. A volunteer is someone who is not necessarily asked, rather he/she steps forward in order to accomplish something. Jesus said there is no greater love than to lay down one's life for his friends. (John 15:13)

~ THE HEART OF AN INTERCESSOR ~
4. MERCY
As in the above list, intercessors stand in the gap for another, seeking mercy instead of judgment, life over death. They are willing to face a risk and sacrifice in order to obtain mercy. (James 2:13)

5. HUMILITY & SERVICE
In each one of these cases, these powerful intercessors wanted to serve those they were interceding for. Their willingness to serve resulted in humility, laying down that which they highly esteemed. (Matt 23:11)

~ THE RELATIONSHIP OF AN INTERCESSOR ~
6. FAVOR
The above role models lived in a place of favor, having a personal and loving relationship with God. They knew what it was to walk and talk with Him, and trust in His goodness. (Prov 12:2)

Others who did not have a personal relationship with Jesus prior to their request, knew His works, listened to His Words, understood His authority and nature. Thus, they anticipated His favor in spite of the risk.

~ THE RESULTS OF AN INTERCESSOR ~
7. MULTIPLIED SEED

Jesus said, "Most assuredly, I say to you, unless a grain of wheat falls into the ground and dies, it remains alone; but if it dies, it produces much grain." (John 12:24 NKJV) The most powerful intercessors, past and present, are ones who have laid down their lives, their dreams, their ambitions, their own personal agendas, everything they have held dear, in order to follow Jesus' footsteps to their own personal cross. The results of such a journey is His promise of multiplication. These intercessors can pray a prayer, make a request, make a stand and have it bear fruit for the masses.

~ WORD STUDY ~

In the Old Testament, the word intercessor comes from the Hebrew word: paga' (paw-gah'):   06293 paga' {paw-gah'} ¤ a primitive root; TWOT - 1731; v

This Hebrew word is translated:
paga`
OT:6293 paga` (paw-gah'); a primitive root; **to impinge**, by accident or violence, or (figuratively) **by importunity**:
KJV - come (betwixt), cause to entreat, fall (upon), make intercession, intercessor, intreat, lay, light [upon], meet (together), pray, reach, run.

In the New Testament, the word intercessor comes from the Greek word (en-toong-khan'-o): (# 1793 entugchano from NT:1722 and NT:5177.
This Greek word means:
to light upon a person or a thing, fall in with, hit upon, a person or a thing 2) to go to or meet a person, esp. for the purpose of conversation, consultation, or supplication 3) to pray, entreat 4) make intercession for any one

14

Scriptures share that He wants our input. He still makes the final decisions, but He listens and what we say can have a part in the outcomes. For those who like to study, here are some additional scriptures saying that God is looking for volunteer intercessors, those willing to lay down their lives for a cause: Isa 64:7, Jer 30:13, Isa 59:16, Jer 27:18, Isa 53:12, Eze 22:30-31, Psalms 106:23.

The Lord is restoring the callings of intercessors to the body of Christ. He is raising up an army of volunteers, who are willing to count THEIR cost because they see what is AT cost. May we answer His call in Jesus Name.

8 PILLARS OF A LIVING INTERCESSOR

A Teaching On the Predominant Gifts of Intercessors

An intercessor may walk their whole life in preparation for one moment in history: for the moment they cast their vote and pray just one prayer. It is like Moses when he interceded for Israel. So intercessors are not necessarily prayer warriors, that pray all the time and thus their volume of prayers is what bears weight in the kingdom. Rather it is their walk in the Lord that bears the weight.

Intercessors are called, but few are chosen to walk in the weightiness of continual miraculous power. To be chosen, is to have gone through the fire and yielded to His Sovereignty through death to self. In the process, also yielding to Him to perfect the character/ alignment of one's body, soul and/or spirit to His image. Katheryn Kulman said, "It cost much. It cost everything. But it's worth the cost!"

PONDERINGS: The pillars of walking and being sustained in this place of intercessory assignments are: Free will, Sacrifice, Faith, Hope, Love, Favor, Peace, Partnership.

These pillars are all gifts from God's grace and measure, so they are not earned nor are they the criteria of being chosen for a task. They grow with each assignment. So these are the marking or gifting of an Intercessor. Here is a brief description of these gifts.

1. Intercessors are Volunteers, the calling is not commanded of them. Each assignment is offered, then accepted by free will with no coercion by God in the offering. But the option is made clear in advance, that there are risks, challenges, and great reward, no matter what.

Isa 6:8-11 NKJV
Also I heard the voice of the Lord, saying: "Whom shall I send, And who will go for Us?" Then I said, "Here am I! Send me." And He said, "Go, and tell this people: 'Keep on hearing, but do not understand; Keep on seeing, but do not perceive.' 10 "Make the heart of this people dull, And their ears heavy, And shut their eyes; Lest they see with their eyes, And hear with their ears, And understand with their heart, And return and be healed." Then I said, "Lord, how long?"

2. Intercessors have the Gift of Giving and receive pleasure in sacrifice, even if bittersweet.

Ps 50:5 NKJV
"Gather My saints together to Me, Those who have made a covenant with Me by sacrifice ."

Isa 53:10-11 NKJV
Yet it pleased the LORD to bruise Him; He has put Him to grief. When You make His soul an offering for sin, He shall see His seed, He shall prolong His days, And the pleasure of the LORD shall prosper in His hand. He shall see the labor of His soul, and be satisfied.

3. Intercessors have Great Faith for breakthrough when in the midst of the sufferings of many loved ones.

1 Sam 30:6-8 NKJV
Now David was greatly distressed, for the people spoke of stoning him, because the soul of all the people was grieved, every man for his sons and his daughters. But David strengthened himself in the LORD his God. Then David said to Abiathar the priest, Ahimelech's son, "Please bring the ephod here to me." And Abiathar brought the ephod to David. 8 So David inquired of the LORD, saying, "Shall I pursue this troop? Shall I overtake them?" And He answered him, "Pursue , for you shall surely overtake them and without fail recover all."

4. Intercessors have Hope enough to visualize the victory, the point of breakthrough. This hope carries them through anything that comes their way, acknowledging that nothing passes by them by accident. That whatever burns was meant to burn and whatever is multiplied is meant for great harvest for many.

Rom 5:3-5 NKJV
And not only that, but we also glory in tribulations , knowing that tribulation produces perseverance; 4 and perseverance, character; and character, hope. 5 Now hope does not disappoint, because the love of God has been poured out in our hearts by the Holy Spirit who was given to us.

5. Intercessors have Stubborn Love. This is God's Fatherly heart for His people, that simply won't quit or change. God's love covers a multitude of sins and it is that love that an intercessor draws upon when the chips are down.

1 Cor 13:7 AMP
Love bears up under anything and everything that comes, is ever ready to believe the best of every person, its hopes are fadeless under all circumstances, and it endures everything [without weakening].

1 Peter 4:7-8 NKJV

But the end of all things is at hand; therefore be serious and watchful in your prayers. And above all things have fervent love for one another, for "love will cover a multitude of sins ."

1 Cor 13 NLT
If I had the gift of prophecy, and if I knew all the mysteries of the future and knew everything about everything, but didn't love others, what good would I be? And if I had the gift of faith so that I could speak to a mountain and make it move, without love I would be no good to anybody. 3 If I gave everything I have to the poor and even sacrificed my body, I could boast about it; but if I didn't love others, I would be of no value whatsoever.

Love is patient and kind. Love is not jealous or boastful or proud 5 or rude. Love does not demand its own way. Love is not irritable, and it keeps no record of when it has been wronged. 6 It is never glad about injustice but rejoices whenever the truth wins out. 7 Love never gives up, never loses faith, is always hopeful, and endures through every circumstance. Love will last forever, but prophecy and speaking in unknown languages and special knowledge will all disappear. 9 Now we know only a little, and even the gift of prophecy reveals little! 10 But when the end comes, these special gifts will all disappear.

It's like this: When I was a child, I spoke and thought and reasoned as a child does. But when I grew up, I put away childish things. 12 Now we see things imperfectly as in a poor mirror, but then we will see everything with perfect clarity. All that I know now is partial and incomplete, but then I will know everything completely, just as God knows me now. 13 There are three things that will endure — faith, hope, and love — and the greatest of these is love.

6. An Intercessor is marked with Great Favor of being daily loaded with benefits. The provision is liberal Favor/ Grace in whatever gift is necessary in heaven and on earth to be able to complete the assignment, stay stable and be kept. The provision is ALWAYS more then enough.

Ezra 7:19-20 NLKV
And whatever more may be needed for the house of your God, which you may have occasion to provide, pay for it from the king's treasury.

7. An Intercessor knows the power of walking in Peace. It requires learning how to daily lean/ abide to find the balance of keeping one's peace in daily living. God's peace is the barometer that holds him stable and when that peace is challenged, the intercessor will do whatever is necessary to re-gain that peace.

Rom 16:19-20 NKJV
For your obedience has become known to all. Therefore I am glad on your behalf; but I want you to be wise in what is good, and simple concerning evil. 20 And the God of peace will crush Satan under your feet shortly. Amen.

8. An Intercessor becomes God's Partner and is willing to express His heart in whatever way He sees fit to express it. The partnership eventually becomes the greatest joy, passion and desire to be able to give pleasure to Him and receive intimacy from Him in the process.

Ex 33:12-17 NLT
Moses said to the LORD, "You have been telling me, 'Take these people up to the Promised Land.' But you haven't told me whom you will send with me. You call me by name and tell me I have found favor with you. 13 Please, if this is really so, show me your intentions so I will understand you more fully and do exactly what you want me to do. Besides, don't forget that this nation is your very own people."

And the LORD replied, "I will personally go with you, Moses. I will give you rest — everything will be fine for you." Then Moses said, "If you don't go with us personally, don't let us move a step from this place. 16 If you don't go with us, how will anyone ever know that your people and I have found favor with you? How else will they know we are special and distinct from all other people on the earth?" And the LORD replied to Moses, "I will indeed do what you have asked, for you have found favor with me, and you are my friend ."

INTERCESSORS ARE PEACE MAKERS

ESTABLISHING MY PEACE: RISE UP TO YOUR PLACES OF AUTHORITY

HEARD 10/15/07: *The glory of God. End times. I do whatever He tells me to do. Obedience.*

DREAM: *I was outside in a school yard, underneath the covered sidewalks. There was a storm in the distance and the sky was angry. I had been told by the Lord to **address the storm, bind it, then command peace** to the storm in Jesus Name. I was very careful in how I took authority over this, knowing it was caused by a principality and I needed to stay obedient to the Lord's command and not directly attack the principality, but instead take authority over its fruit which was the storm.*

Mark 4:38-41 NKJV
...Teacher, do You not care that we are perishing?" Then He arose and rebuked the wind, and said to the sea, "Peace, be still!" And the wind ceased and there was a great calm. But He said to them, "Why are you so fearful? How is it that you have no faith?" And they feared exceedingly, and said to one another, "Who can this be, that even the wind and the sea obey Him!"

Col 1:15-18 NKJV
He is the image of the invisible God, the firstborn over all creation. For by Him all things were created that are in heaven and that are on earth, visible and invisible, whether thrones or dominions or principalities or powers. All things were created through Him and for Him. And He is before all things, and in Him all things consist.

20

HEARD: *Build a shield a faith. That is what it is all about. Canopy. Covered. Rice paddies. Hurricane. Despondent. New crop. Why am I telling you this? So that you will pray.*

QUICKENED MEMORY SCRIPTURE:
Matt 5:13-16 NKJV
"You are the salt of the earth; but if the salt loses its flavor, how shall it be seasoned? It is then good for nothing but to be thrown out and trampled underfoot by men. "You are the light of the world. A city that is set on a hill cannot be hidden. Nor do they light a lamp and put it under a basket, but on a lampstand, and it gives light to all who are in the house. Let your light so shine before men, that they may see your good works and glorify your Father in heaven.

HEARD: *Alliance.*

WORD TO PONDER: BIND THE STORMS AND LOOSE PEACE 10/15/07

Dear Intercessors, listen to the pleas of the vulnerable. In one storm, an entire livelihood can be demolished and much suffering result. Rise up, gather in an alliance of faith and pray for those in need. These children do not have salt they need to preserve them. The righteous, they are the salt that preserves the earth and the inhabitants thereof.

Rise to your callings, your places and establish My good and peaceful domain. This hour the enemy seeks to bring the ravages of war, fear and unrest to all, for he knows his time is short and My kingdom rule will be established upon the earth through My children. There will come a day when the nursing child shall play with the cobra and none shall hurt for the knowledge of Me shall cover the earth even as the waters cover the sea. In that day you will walk in the fullness of your position as My sons and My abiding place shall be glorious.

Isa 11:1-10 NKJV
There shall come forth a Rod from the stem of Jesse, And a Branch shall grow out of his roots. 2 The Spirit of the LORD shall rest upon Him, The Spirit of wisdom and understanding, The Spirit of counsel and might, The Spirit of knowledge and of the fear of the LORD.

His delight is in the fear of the LORD, And He shall not judge by the sight of His eyes,Nor decide by the hearing of His ears; 4 But with righteousness He shall judge the poor, And decide with equity for the meek of the earth; He shall strike the earth with the rod of His mouth,And with the breath of His lips He shall slay the wicked. 5 Righteousness shall be the belt of His loins, And faithfulness the belt of His waist.

"The wolf also shall dwell with the lamb ,The leopard shall lie down with the young goat, The calf and the young lion and the fatling together; And a little child shall lead them. 7 The cow and the bear shall graze; Their young ones shall lie down together; And the lion shall eat straw like the ox. 8 The nursing child shall play by the cobra's hole, And the weaned child shall put his hand in the viper's den. 9 They shall not hurt nor destroy in all My holy mountain, For the earth shall be full of the knowledge of the LORD As the waters cover the sea. 10 "And in that day there shall be a Root of Jesse, Who shall stand as a banner to the people; For the Gentiles shall seek Him, And His resting place shall be glorious."

Matt 5:13-16 NKJV
"You are the salt of the earth; but if the salt loses its flavor, how shall it be seasoned? It is then good for nothing but to be thrown out and trampled underfoot by men. "You are the light of the world. A city that is set on a hill cannot be hidden. Nor do they light a lamp and put it under a basket, but on a lampstand, and it gives light to all who are in the house. Let your light so shine before men, that they may see your good works and glorify your Father in heaven.

"He will even deliver one who is not innocent; yes, he will be delivered by the purity of your hands." (Job 22:30 NKJV)

"And he saw that there was no man, and wondered that there was no intercessor: therefore his arm brought salvation unto him; and his righteousness, it sustained him." (Isa 59:16 KJV)

WORD TO PONDER: MY PEACEMAKERS, MY ADVOCATES 2/04/08

My peacemakers are intercessors, standing between the rendings of what is derision. They refuse to let go and wrestle with the contention of what they see does not line up with My Word. These are My beloved ones who do not like confrontation and yet when enflamed by My passion, they will pursue straight to the rending and defend My truth until they see resolution and find peace in their souls that I have heard their advocacy and will rule upon their request.

They have learned that their defense is not caught in the strivings between men. Their defense is in knowing their authority and identity in Me. These are those who will crush satan under their feet, by knowing their God of peace. These are My sons who will rule and reign in My kingdom.

Matt 5:9 NKJV
Blessed are the peacemakers, For they shall be called sons of God.

Luke 1:76-80 NKJV
"And you, child, will be called the prophet of the Highest; For you will go before the face of the Lord to prepare His ways, To give knowledge of salvation to His people By the remission of their sins, Through the tender mercy of our God, With which the Dayspring from on high has visited us; To give light to those who sit in darkness and the shadow of death, To guide our feet into the way of peace ." So the child grew and became strong in spirit, and was in the deserts till the day of his manifestation to Israel.

Rom 16:19-20 NKJV
I want you to be wise in what is good, and simple concerning evil. And the God of peace will crush Satan under your feet shortly.

INTERCESSORS ARE LIKE BAROMETERS

A Teaching on Intercession and Tangible Feelings

I would like to share something the Lord taught me in connection with intercession. Hopefully, this knowledge will help us feel more comfortable in being used by the Lord and keep us from being led astray in our intercessory experiences.

A barometer is a gauge (like an outward sign) that tells us the pressure of the air around us. Intercessors are like barometers. They can walk into a room and their meters will detect things unseen to the natural eye. Part of their gifting is an intuitive sensitivity to a world that most people don't even know exists. As they remain keenly aware of the Holy Spirit's presence and learn to take what they are sensing to prayer, they grow in their giftings and become even more sensitive. These unique experiences are often misunderstood and yet God uses them as signs.

Since 1994, there has been a call by God to raise up new crops of intercessors, to help birth His new thing upon the earth. His strong, near Presence has caused many to fervently respond. Some have matured and are coming into a new level of gifting. The Lord is wanting to enlarge their gifts and further hone their sensitivity for a hands on ministry.

Hebrews says, *"For we have not an high priest which cannot BE TOUCHED WITH THE FEELING OF OUR INFIRMITIES; but was in all points tempted like as we are, yet without sin.*

Let us therefore come boldly unto the throne of grace, that we may obtain mercy, and find grace to help in time of need." (Heb 4:15-16 KJV)

That sentence is a little hard to understand because it is written as a double negative. In the positive, it is saying that Jesus WAS/IS touched with the feeling of our infirmities. The Holy Spirit quickened that verse as I was thinking about the tangible feelings that come with many intercessory experiences. The phrase, "be touched with the feeling of" is actually one Greek word, sumpatheo. (Strongs 4834) It means to feel sympathy or commiserate. I traced that word back to it roots and found something quite interesting. It comes from 2 words meaning to companion or associate with an experience, sensation or impression, usually painful. (Strongs 4862 & 3958) Now that is an interesting definition for those touched by intercession that is birthed by the Holy Spirit! They have experienced this as very real.

We are called to be like Jesus, Who is the greatest Intercessor. As intercessors, we will sometimes feel physical things in our bodies, or experience emotional sensations, and have instinctive impressions of either the room we are in, or the person/ issue we are praying for. This is not supposed to be a unique experience, this is actually the very heart of intercession — to feel and know what touches God's heart. He feels these things and we are allowed brief moments to companion with Him in prayer.

Some call these experiences words of knowledge, some call them discernment, some call them warfare, some call them intercession, some call it responding to His Presence. Actually this gift is all of the above. Some may feel various physical infirmities or pain in their body. Some may sense anger, lust, fear, anxiety, ambition, impatience, joy, peace, compassion, etc. Some may sense a coldness in the room, or heat, or a gentle wind, or slight tingles in their hands, or on their head, or any number of experiences.

Human beings naturally feel all of these things. The **difference for intercessors is that they do not own these feelings**. <u>It is a sudden download, whether strong or gentle, it is a happening that in one minute it is there and another it is not</u>. It is connected with a sensitivity to the Holy Spirit, to the person we are in proximity with, to someone placed upon our heart, or to the environment in a room, etc.

For years I had warfare experiences without understanding why. Several years ago the Lord opened my eyes. As I was driving on the way to see a person, one minute I was worshipping the Lord and the next minute my heart was racing, my stomach gripping and my breathing short. It was such an unusual feeling and I wondered what it was. I asked the Lord and I suddenly realized it was fear. Now that may sound strange, but I was not used to having fear and so it took a while to register that was what I was feeling. It was ridiculously out of context because I was worshipping the Lord, having no worries and it was a nice day!

I bound the spirit of fear, commanded it to go in Jesus Name and was flooded with peace. As I was pulling into the driveway, I was still scratching my head wondering why I would suddenly be attacked like that, but at least I knew it was a demon. When I walked in I noticed that the lady was kind of white faced. She was holding onto the counter and I asked her if she was OK. She told me she had just had a panic attack. I asked her how long ago, and it was exactly when I'd experienced this. That was a real eye opener. The Lord allowed me to experience this, so that as I warred, she would be set free from that attack!

There is a deception that can happen in this area of experiencing these tangible feelings. When Jesus hung on the cross, He bore everything upon Himself, so that we do not have to. The scripture says, *"Surely He has BORNE our griefs and CARRIED our sorrows; yet we esteemed Him stricken, smitten by God, and afflicted. But He was wounded for our transgressions, He was bruised for our iniquities; The chastisement for our peace was upon Him, and by His stripes we are healed. All we like sheep have gone astray; We have turned, every one, to his own way; And the Lord has LAID ON HIM the iniquity of us all." (Isa 53:4-6 NKJV)*

The difference is that as intercessors we are not meant to CARRY any of these experiences. **We can be TOUCHED by the feelings, but we are not to BEAR them. If we do, we take Jesus' place on the cross**. I had noticed a few intercessors living with their burdens, and as I was praying about this, the Lord told me it was a spirit of delusion whose name was savior! So if you have been carrying someone else's pain, or someone else's warfare, start rebuking it in Jesus Name. Do not own it, do not carry it, do not accept it, do not embrace it, do not receive it.

In contrast, when we are touched by the heart of God and experience tangible feelings, it is for the express purpose of giving them back to Him. He touches us, so that we can yield them up to Him in prayer. He touches us so that we can understand what is going on, and take authority over it, so that the enemy does not have his way.

Another common error is that when we experience these tangible things, we begin to think that we are the ones with the problems. The enemy would love to make us think this. If he convinces us, then he has two victims, the person with the problem and then us - because we receive it through our belief! Therefore, we must learn to not take the things we experience personally. The Lord wants to hone our sensitivity so that we will stand against the enemy, we will pray, and we will minister to others in His Name.

Another error that often takes place is an intercessor's personal response after being a public sign or gauge. Sometimes they feel shame because it was a public display and they are embarrassed. That is because pride and servanthood are not compatible! Following Jesus to the cross, we learn that to be a servant is the lowliest of all. The beauty of this is that such intercessors so love the Presence of the Lord that they gladly sacrifice all for just one touch of His Presence. They so love the Presence of the Lord, they long for that, and that is the only place they want to be.

Lord, please hone our sensitivity to these gifts so that we can lay hands on the hurting and heal them and set them free in Jesus Name. And help us to remember the battle belongs to You. (2 Chron 20:15)

~~~~~~~~~~

QUESTIONS AND ANSWERS ABOUT INTERCESSORY BAROMETERS

[Questions from readers and answers from Sandy]

Question: I was wondering if you could give me an example of the way to pray when one feels what another person is going through. I have felt this and had the feeling that this was what the other person was going through.

Answer:
When I feel the emotions of what someone is feeling, I might ask the person, "Is this the way you are feeling?" If I am correct, I pray what I am feeling, knowing this is an expression of their heart. I might say something like this: "Lord, she feels lost and lonely and confused. And I sense she has wanted to receive more from You for so long, but does not know how to reach You. She feels disconnected. Please bring her the comfort she needs and let her know how much You love her." If it is appropriate, I might bind any spirits of rejection, confusion and isolation and break them off in Jesus Name. When someone realizes that you just spoke out exactly how they are feeling, it is like a mirror to them and helps them to realize that they are NOT alone.

28

When we feel what they are feeling, it brings comfort and understanding that the Lord also knows exactly how they are feeling.

~~~~~~~~~~

Question: I have just been in prayer for and about two recent tragedies in other's lives. I felt later that I could have prayed differently and that they might be alive today. I wondered how do you deal with these situations in your life and ministry?

Answer:
There are many scriptures in the Old and New Testaments that say we are to give according to our ability. The Lord is very grateful for whatever portion we share of our hearts and lives. If we remember what we missed later on, then we were simply not given the whole revelation at the time. The Lord is not holding us responsible for what we didn't have and doesn't want us to feel guilty and condemned about it.

2 Cor 8:12 NLT
Give whatever you can according to what you have. If you are really eager to give, it isn't important how much you are able to give. God wants you to give what you have, not what you don't have.
~~~~~~~~~~

Question: How can I tell if what I am feeling is myself or intercession?

Answer:
The way I tell if what I am feeling is intercession versus myself is to check my own thoughts and circumstances. If the feeling is foreign to where I am at the time, (via thoughts, circumstances, conversations, etc) then it is pretty obvious that what I am feeling is a portion of what someone else is fighting. If I am wrong and this is something that is my own

problem, either way the answer is the same, and that is to pray and war until it is gone.

I have had several ask this same question about discerning. For me, the answer has to do with whether I am in the room with other people, whether I have laid hands upon someone, whether I have someone on my heart at the time, or whether the Lord has given me an intercessory assignment.

~~~~~~~~~~~

Question: What does this scripture mean? "Bear one another's burdens, and so fulfill the law of Christ." (Gal 6:2)

Answer:
According to the Greek, it means we mend a sinner by removing his weight. (But not carrying the weight ourselves.)

In context, Gal 6:2 is speaking about restoring someone who has been overtaken in a trespass. According to the Greek language, the person has been overtaken in sin, and we are to literally "mend or repair" such a person. We do so, by "lifting through the idea of removal" the weight or load off their shoulders of being overtaken in sin.

In the following study of the Greek word "bear", **it does not mean to lift off someone else so that we can live with it ourselves. It means to REMOVE the weight**. There is a false doctrine that suggests we carry sicknesses in our own body so that others do not have to, or so that we can be martyrs in their stead. When I saw this going on in several intercessory people, they were living with the things that they were lifting off someone else. The Lord clearly expressed to me that this was coming from a spirit called "false savior" where they were taking Jesus' place.

Gal 6:1-3 NLT

Dear brothers and sisters, if another Christian is overcome by some sin, you who are godly should gently and humbly help that person back onto the right path. And be careful not to fall into the same temptation yourself. 2 Share each other's troubles and problems, and in this way obey the law of Christ. 3 If you think you are too important to help someone in need, you are only fooling yourself. You are really a nobody.

Gal 6:1-5 NAS
6:1 Brethren, even if a man is caught in any trespass, you who are spiritual, restore such a one in a spirit of gentleness; each one looking to yourself, lest you too be tempted. 2 Bear one another's burdens, and thus fulfill the law of Christ. 3 For if anyone thinks he is something when he is nothing, he deceives himself. 4 But let each one examine his own work, and then he will have reason for boasting in regard to himself alone, and not in regard to another. 5 For each one shall bear his own load.

Gal 6:1-5 NKJV
6:1 Brethren, if a man is overtaken in any trespass, you who are spiritual restore [2675] such a one in a spirit of gentleness, considering yourself lest you also be tempted. 2 Bear [941] one another's burdens [922], and so fulfill the law of Christ. 3 For if anyone thinks himself to be something, when he is nothing, he deceives himself. 4 But let each one examine his own work, and then he will have rejoicing in himself alone, and not in another. 5 For each one shall bear his own load.

RESTORE
NT:2675
katartizo (kat-ar-tid'-zo); from NT:2596 and a derivative of NT:739; to complete thoroughly, i.e. repair (literally or figuratively) or adjust:
KJV - fit, frame, mend, (make) perfect (-ly join together), prepare, restore.

BURDENS
NT:922
baros (bar'-os); probably from the same as NT:939 (through the notion of going down; compare NT:899); weight; in the N. T. only figuratively, a load, abundance, authority:
KJV - burden (-some), weight.

BEAR YE
NT:941
bastazo (bas-tad'-zo); perhaps remotely derived from the base of NT:939 (through the idea of removal); to lift, literally or figuratively
~~~~~~~~~~~

Question: Is the scripture on "knowing the fellowship of His sufferings" about intercession? *"That I may know him, and the power of his resurrection, and the fellowship of his sufferings, being made conformable unto his death; If by any means I might attain unto the resurrection of the dead." (Phil 3:10 -11 KJV)*

Answer:
This scripture is speaking about Christ's sufferings on earth, not about His sufferings of intercession in heaven.

In Phil 3:10 the context and focus of this entire section of scripture is talking about partnering with the same sufferings Jesus had on earth, not the sufferings of intercession He is now in heaven.

The Greek word used for sufferings in Phil 3:10 is used 16 times in the New Testament. In every case, this is speaking about suffering on earth.

(Rom 7:5, Rom 8:18, 2 Cor 1:5, 2 Cor 1:6, 2 Cor 1:7, Gal 5:24, Phil 3:10, Col 1:24, 2 Tim 3:11, Heb 2:9, Heb 2:10,

Heb 10:32, 1 Peter 1:11, 1 Peter 4:13, 1 Peter 5:1, 1 Peter 5:9)

Example: *"For I consider that the sufferings of this present time are not worthy to be compared with the glory which shall be revealed in us." (Rom 8:18-19 NKJV)*

So if this is not about intercession, what IS that section of scripture talking about? Let us look at this section of scripture in context. Previously, Paul has just stated a case where he had every reason to trust in his flesh. Then he expresses that these things are but garbage, because he understands that to die to self (on earth) and all his human qualifications of self righteousness is to gain the resurrection (which is in heaven.)

In these 2 verses, Paul is speaking about knowing Christ, Who was resurrected to heaven after He suffered and died on earth. He says that to know Christ is to experience the same things He experienced, which was suffering on earth for sharing His testimony about His Father and kingdom, yielding His life to the cross because His Father asked Him to and then being resurrected from death and taken into His heavenly kingdom to rule and reign.

Paul is speaking about dying to self and suffering loss on earth so that in the end he can be resurrected to heaven just like Jesus was. All through the gospels, Jesus speaks about death to self. It is a daily process of laying down our own desires and strengths for His sake, and following in the footsteps of Jesus. Jesus suffered on earth and all through the gospels He promises us the same suffering while on earth. When we have fellowship with Jesus, we are partnering with Him in the same sufferings He also suffered while on earth.

Phil 3:3-6 NLT

We put no confidence in human effort. Instead, we boast about what Christ Jesus has done for us. 4 Yet I could have confidence in myself if anyone could. If others have reason for confidence in their own efforts, I have even more! 5 For I was circumcised when I was eight days old, having been born into a pure-blooded Jewish family that is a branch of the tribe of Benjamin. So I am a real Jew if there ever was one! What's more, I was a member of the Pharisees, who demand the strictest obedience to the Jewish law. 6 And zealous? Yes, in fact, I harshly persecuted the church. And I obeyed the Jewish law so carefully that I was never accused of any fault.

Phil 3:7-11 NLT
7 I once thought all these things were so very important, but now I consider them worthless because of what Christ has done. 8 Yes, everything else is worthless when compared with the priceless gain of knowing Christ Jesus my Lord. I have discarded everything else, counting it all as garbage, so that I may have Christ 9 and become one with him. I no longer count on my own goodness or my ability to obey God's law, but I trust Christ to save me. For God's way of making us right with himself depends on faith. 10 As a result, I can really know Christ and experience the mighty power that raised him from the dead. I can learn what it means to suffer with him, sharing in his death, 11 so that, somehow, I can experience the resurrection from the dead!

Phil 3:10 -11 KJV
10 That I may know him, and the power of his resurrection, and the fellowship of his sufferings, being made conformable unto his death; 11 If by any means I might attain unto the resurrection of the dead.

SUFFERINGS
NT:3804

pathema (path'-ay-mah); from a presumed derivative of NT:3806; something undergone, i.e. hardship or pain; subjectively, an emotion or influence:
KJV - affection, affliction, motion, suffering.

NT:3806
pathos (path'-os); from the alternate of NT:3958; properly, suffering ("pathos"), i.e. (subjectively) a passion (especially concupiscence):
KJV - (inordinate) affection, lust.

That word for sufferings comes from a Greek word that we get our English word pathos from. This root word [pathos 3806] is recorded 42 times in the New Testament. This suffering was also an earthly suffering in the flesh.

NT:3958
pascho (pas'-kho); including the forms (patho (path'-o) and pentho (pen'-tho)), used only in certain tenses for it; apparently a primary verb; to experience a sensation or impression (usually painful):
KJV - feel, passion, suffer, vex.

(Matt 16:21, Matt 17:12, Matt 17:15, Matt 27:19, Mark 5:26, Mark 8:31, Mark 9:12, Luke 9:22, Luke 13:2, Luke 17:25, Luke 22:15, Luke 24:26, Luke 24:46, Acts 1:3, Acts 3:18, Acts 9:16, Acts 17:3, Acts 28:5, 1 Cor 12:26, 2 Cor 1:6, Gal 3:4, Phil 1:29, 1 Thess 2:14, 2 Thess 1:5, 2 Tim 1:12, Heb 2:18, Heb 5:8, Heb 9:26, Heb 13:12, 1 Peter 2:19, 1 Peter 2:20, 1 Peter 2:21, 1 Peter 2:23, 1 Peter 3:14, 1 Peter 3:17, 1 Peter 3:18, 1 Peter 4:1, 1 Peter 4:1, 1 Peter 4:15, 1 Peter 4:19, 1 Peter 5:10, Rev 2:10)
Out of these 42 scriptures that use the word suffer, 21 times speak directly about Christ's suffering on earth.

Mark 8:31 NKJV
31 And He began to teach them that the Son of Man must SUFFER [3958] many things, and be rejected by the elders

35

and chief priests and scribes, and be killed, and after three days rise again.

1 Peter 3:18 NKJV
18 For Christ also SUFFERED [3958] once for sins, the just for the unjust, that He might bring us to God, being put to death in the flesh but made alive by the Spirit.

~~~~~~~~~~

Question: Is the scripture about filling up that which is behind in the afflictions of Christ in my flesh, about intercession?   "Who now rejoice in my sufferings for you, and fill up that which is behind of the afflictions [2347] of Christ in my flesh for his body's sake, which is the church:" (Col 1:24 KJV)

Answer:
The phrase to "fill up that which is behind of the afflictions" is speaking about fulfilling the promises of Jesus that we will suffer tribulations. Jesus spoke many promises that we would suffer and Paul was saying they had not all yet been fulfilled.

The Greek word translated afflictions in this scripture comes from many layers of words. In each case, it is obvious to me that these are afflictions through living in this world under the weight of demonic territory. These are pressures, anguish, burdens, persecutions, tribulations, trouble, crowding, thronging, woundings, crushings.
This same Greek word [#2347] is mentioned 45 times in the New Testament.

[Matt 13:21, Matt 24:9, Matt 24:21, Matt 24:29, Mark 4:17, Mark 13:19, Mark 13:24, John 16:21, John 16:33, Acts 7:10, Acts 7:11, Acts 11:19, Acts 14:22, Acts 20:23, Rom 2:9, Rom 5:3, Rom 5:3, Rom 8:35, Rom 12:12, 1 Cor 7:28, 2 Cor 1:4, 2 Cor 1:4, 2 Cor 1:8, 2 Cor 2:4, 2 Cor 4:17, 2 Cor 6:4, 2

Cor 7:4, 2 Cor 8:2, 2 Cor 8:13, Eph 3:13, Phil 1:17, Phil 4:14, Col 1:24, 1 Thess 1:6, 1 Thess 3:3, 1 Thess 3:7, 2 Thess 1:4, 2 Thess 1:6, Heb 10:33, James 1:27, Rev 1:9, Rev 2:9, Rev 2:10, Rev 2:22, Rev 7:14]

Here are some of those verses and notice that in these verses, these are <u>promises of afflictions or tribulations yet to come</u>. So the lack that Paul is speaking of in Col 1:24 are the promised pressures, anguish, burdens, persecutions, tribulations, trouble, crowding, thronging, woundings, crushings not yet fulfilled.

Matt 24:9 KJV
Then shall they deliver you up to be afflicted [2347], and shall kill you: and ye shall be hated of all nations for my name's sake.

Matt 24:21 KJV
For then shall be great tribulation [2347], such as was not since the beginning of the world to this time, no, nor ever shall be.

Matt 24:29 KJV
Immediately after the tribulation [2347] of those days shall the sun be darkened, and the moon shall not give her light, and the stars shall fall from heaven, and the powers of the heavens shall be shaken:

John 16:33 KJV
These things I have spoken unto you, that in me ye might have peace. In the world ye shall have tribulation [2347]: but be of good cheer; I have overcome the world.

Acts 14:22 KJV
Confirming the souls of the disciples, and exhorting them to continue in the faith, and that we must through much tribulation [2347] enter into the kingdom of God.

Rev 2:9-10 NKJV
9 "I know your works, tribulation [2347], and poverty (but you are rich); and I know the blasphemy of those who say they are Jews and are not, but are a synagogue of Satan. 10 Do not fear any of those things which you are about to suffer.

Rev 7:14 NKJV
14 And I said to him, "Sir, you know." So he said to me, "These are the ones who come out of the great tribulation [2347], and washed their robes and made them white in the blood of the Lamb.

AFFLICTIONS
NT:2347
thlipsis (thlip'-sis); from NT:2346; pressure (literally or figuratively):
KJV - afflicted (-tion), anguish, burdened, persecution, tribulation, trouble.

NT:2346
thlibo (thlee'-bo); akin to the base of NT:5147; to crowd (literally or figuratively):
KJV - afflict, narrow, throng, suffer tribulation, trouble.

NT:5147
tribos (tree'-bos); from tribo (to "rub"; akin to teiro, truo, and the base of NT:5131, NT:5134); a rut or worn track:
KJV - path.

NT:5134
trauma (trow'-mah); from the base of titrosko (to wound; akin to the base of NT:2352, NT:5147, NT:5149, etc.); a wound:
KJV - wound.
NT:2352
thrauo (throw'-o); a primary verb; to crush:
KJV - bruise. Compare NT:4486.

NT:5147

tribos (tree'-bos); from tribo (to "rub"; akin to teiro, truo, and the base of NT:5131, NT:5134); a rut or worn track: KJV - path.

NT:5149
trizo (trid'-zo); apparently a primary verb; to creak (squeak), i.e. (by analogy) to grate the teeth (in frenzy): KJV - gnash.

Fill up
NT:466
antanapleroo (an-tan-ap-lay-ro'-o); from NT:473 and NT:378; to supplement: KJV - fill up.

NT:378
anapleroo (an-ap-lay-ro'-o); from NT:303 and NT:4137; to complete; by implication, to occupy, supply; figuratively, to accomplish (by coincidence ot obedience): KJV - fill up, fulfill, occupy, supply.

NT:4137
pleroo (play-ro'-o); from NT:4134; to make replete, i.e. (literally) to cram (a net), level up (a hollow), or (figuratively) to furnish (or imbue, diffuse, influence), satisfy, execute (an office), finish (a period or task), verify (or coincide with a prediction), etc.: KJV - accomplish, X after, (be) complete, end, expire, fill (up), fulfil, (be, make) full (come), fully preach, perfect, supply.

~~~~~~~~~~

Question: If "fill up" means the unfulfilled promises of suffering (as in the above study) then why did Paul say his suffering was for the body of Christ? "Who now rejoice in my sufferings for you, and fill up that which is behind of the afflictions of Christ in my flesh for his body's sake, which is the church:" (Col 1:24 KJV)

Answer:

Because there are two causes of suffering. One kind of suffering is suffering for the Lord's sake, the other is for the sake of ministering the gospel. Paul spoke of sufferings from laboring as a minister of the gospel, for the sake of God's people.

If you read the same scripture in context, you will notice below that Paul claims 4 times that he is suffering for the people of God because he is a minister to them. There are many scriptures where Paul makes it clear that his sufferings on earth are for those he loves and serves, not only for the Lord Jesus, but for His body which is the church.

Now read it in context:

Col 1:24-29 NKJV

24 I now rejoice in my sufferings FOR YOU, and fill up in my flesh what is lacking in the afflictions of Christ, FOR THE SAKE OF HIS BODY, which is THE CHURCH, 25 of which I became a minister according to the stewardship from God which was given to me FOR YOU, to fulfill the word of God, 26 the mystery which has been hidden from ages and from generations, but now has been revealed to His saints. 27 To them God willed to make known what are the riches of the glory of this mystery among the Gentiles: which is Christ in you, the hope of glory. 28 Him we preach, warning every man and teaching every man in all wisdom, THAT WE MAY PRESENT EVERY MAN PERFECT IN CHRIST JESUS. 29 TO THIS END I ALSO LABOR, striving according to His working which works in me mightily.

Eph 3:1-2 NKJV

3:1 For this reason I, Paul, the prisoner of Christ Jesus FOR YOU GENTILES —

Eph 3:13 NKJV
13 Therefore I ask that you do not lose heart at MY TRIBULATIONS FOR YOU, which is your glory.

Phil 2:17-18 NKJV
17 Yes, and if I am being poured out as a drink offering on the SACRIFICE AND SERVICE OF YOUR FAITH, I am glad and rejoice with you all. 18 For the same reason you also be glad and rejoice with me.

2 Tim 2:10 NKJV
10 Therefore I endure all things FOR THE SAKE OF THE ELECT, that they also may obtain the salvation which is in Christ Jesus with eternal glory.

Matt 5:11 KJV
11 Blessed are ye, when men shall revile you, and persecute you, and shall say all manner of evil against you falsely, FOR MY SAKE.

Acts 5:41 KJV
41 And they departed from the presence of the council, rejoicing that they were counted worthy to suffer shame FOR HIS NAME.

INTERCESSORS EXPRESS GODLY LONGINGS

HEARD 7/09/04: *May we always be able to move into answered prayers. Yearning to move. Forward into destiny. To be held back no longer. Open up the life line. Pray like your life depended upon it. Do you see the difference? Passion. Prayers moves Me, like it moves you.*

Being moved by faith. It has do to with pressing in. And moving it to earth. It's calling forth that which belongs here. Yes truth. Prayer is My key. My mystery. Canopy. See it like it is, through prayer. I'll be here to hear you. Multiply it back on earth where it belongs. Passion, it's what you are feeling.

Mourning. Mourning over the condition of My bride. I want her healed. She's My treasure. Always will be.

Your part matters. It's how I operate. Must be birthed and announced. To come full circle. Birthed through prayer. Announcement. I want you with Me, by My side. Undaunted. To put it into My Words. Holy yearning.

PIX: *I saw things being downloaded in a channel.*

HEARD: *A channel. What is My joy? To see you moving. Oppression break it off. Heaviness. Sorrow. What is the way above it? To pray for release. And there you have it, done. And keep on ruling on earth.*

=======

HEARD 2/04/08 : *My peacemaker. Deliverer. You are gentle. The very essence of the longing. Who you are. Why you have written much on the subject. It is your intercession sweetheart, to be one.*

My pleasure. My passion. Raising children. It's more than just a map.

1 Thess 2:7-9 NKJV
But we were gentle among you, just as a nursing mother cherishes her own children. So, affectionately longing for you, we were well pleased to impart to you not only the gospel of God, but also our own lives, because you had become dear to us.

WORD TO PONDER: DESTINY: THE VERY ESSENCE OF LONGING 2/04/08

I have heard your cries for the vision, the map of destiny on behalf of what you labor. I understand your desire for sight, but what I have given you is much deeper than that. The very essence of your spiritual DNA is deeply embedded into the fiber of your existence in Me. Just as My Spirit groans without words, what I have engrained inside of you is without language. It is being one with Me and carrying what I carry as you walk it out on earth. This is the very heart of intercession.

Remember that wisdom is justified by her children. The fruit of your labors is your children. Your groanings are birthing on earth what is spoken from heaven over your life. You can not help but follow the seed of passion I planted in you. And you will conquer anything that keeps you from walking in the peace and fulfillment of what you long for in Me.

Gal 4:19-20 NKJV
... My little children, for whom I labor in birth again until Christ is formed in you.

Rom 8:21-27 NKJV
For we know that the whole creation groans and labors with birth pangs together until now. 23 Not only that, but we also who have the firstfruits of the Spirit, even we ourselves groan within ourselves, eagerly waiting for the adoption, the redemption of our body. 24 For we were saved in this hope, but hope that is seen is not hope; for why does one still hope for what he sees? 25 But if we hope for what we do not see, we eagerly wait for it with perseverance. 26 Likewise the Spirit also helps in our weaknesses. For we do not know what we should pray for as we ought, but the Spirit Himself makes intercession for us with groanings which cannot be uttered. 27 Now He who searches the hearts knows what the mind of the Spirit is, because He makes intercession for the saints according to the will of God.

John 11:33-39 NKJV
Therefore, when Jesus saw her weeping, and the Jews who came with her weeping, He groaned in the spirit and was

troubled. *34 And He said, "Where have you laid him?" They said to Him, "Lord, come and see." 35 Jesus wept. 36 Then the Jews said, "See how He loved him!" 37 And some of them said, "Could not this Man, who opened the eyes of the blind, also have kept this man from dying?" Then Jesus, again groaning in Himself, came to the tomb. It was a cave, and a stone lay against it. 39 Jesus said, "Take away the stone."*

Acts 7:33-34 NKJV
'Then the LORD said to him, "Take your sandals off your feet, for the place where you stand is holy ground. 34 I have surely seen the oppression of My people who are in Egypt; I have heard their groaning and have come down to deliver them. And now come, I will send you to Egypt."'

2 Cor 5:2-5 NKJV
For in this we groan, earnestly desiring to be clothed with our habitation which is from heaven, 3 if indeed, having been clothed, we shall not be found naked. 4 For we who are in this tent groan , being burdened, not because we want to be unclothed, but further clothed, that mortality may be swallowed up by life. 5 Now He who has prepared us for this very thing is God, who also has given us the Spirit as a guarantee.

WORD TO PONDER LISTEN TO MY YEARNINGS 3/12/97
I have set My mark upon you and I have set you as My sign to touch the world around you. Part of recognizing this is listening to your yearnings. My Spirit is within you and draws you by those special yearnings in your heart.

"To whom God would make known what is the riches of the glory of this mystery among the Gentiles; which is Christ in you, the hope of glory." (Col 1:27 KJV)

WORD TO PONDER: HOLY FIRE 3/9/98

A fire is building. Watch the flames flicker with each gust of wind. As I breathe upon My people, the wind takes hold of each ember to burst forth new flames of kindled heat. Watch the fire. It grows hotter as each hour passes. Watch it build, as My people return to their first love.... The flames of passion from My people grow, as they worship Me with all of their strength... The glow of desire becomes more intense as they seek Me with all their hearts... The luminescence of their minds electrifies as they hunger for My Words. The flame grows hotter. The passion deepens.

My people, who stir My heart. My people, who draw out My great longings to respond to your unabashed love. Call on Me and I will answer! Seek Me and I will be found. The cloud of My Presence will descend upon the earth and you will be found in Me for I dwell in the praises of My people. I long to dwell in the midst of your fiery passion. Let the fires burn. Let them burn deeply.

"For our God is a consuming fire." (Hebrews 12:29)

"And ye shall seek Me, and find Me, when ye shall search for Me with all your heart." (Jeremiah 29:13)

"Thou hast ravished my heart, my sister, my spouse; thou hast ravished my heart with one of thine eyes, with one chain of thy neck." (Song of Solomon 4:9)

THE HEART OF PRAYER

When we are stirred by His heart of compassion, we suddenly see each precious life as a lamb.... weak, vulnerable... needy and lacking.

Spiritual gifts and knowledge do not make a man great. Compassion makes a great man.

Mark 6:34-35 NKJV
And Jesus, when He came out, saw a great multitude and was moved with compassion for them, because they were like sheep not having a shepherd. So He began to teach them many things.

PART TWO:
TYPES OF INTERCESSIONS

Intercession is Repentance

WHAT TO DO ABOUT JUDGMENT

VISION 6/12/07: *I saw Bobby Conner was in a store and talking to a lady. She was talking about a volcano and he said, "You know that is going to go off, don't you?" She said yes, and he said, "Well what can we do about it?"*

I had overheard the conversation and in answer to Bobby's question I bellowed loudly from the depths of my intercessory being, "STOP!! STOP SINNING! PRAY, PRAY, PRAY!!!!"

2 Chron 7:13-17 NKJV
When I shut up heaven and there is no rain, or command the locusts to devour the land, or send pestilence among My people, 14 if My people who are called by My name will humble themselves, and pray and seek My face, and turn from their wicked ways, then I will hear from heaven, and will forgive their sin and heal their land. 15 Now My eyes will be open and My ears attentive to prayer made in this place. 16 For now I have chosen and sanctified this house, that My name may be there forever; and My eyes and My heart will be there perpetually.

HOW TO RESTORE CHURCH POWER

HEARD 3/14/08: *Naked.*

PIX: *I saw the action of pulling off a piece of clothing over someone's head.*

Rev 16:15 NKJV
"Behold, I am coming as a thief. Blessed is he who watches, and keeps his garments, lest he walk naked and they see his shame."

HEARD: *Restoring church power. How do we do that? Obedience to scripture. Come beloveds, repent with Me. I came to restore you into alignment.*

PIX: *I saw a folded white linen garment that was being handed over to a person.*

HEARD: *Show them how. Tell it like it is. Find the equation. Do you have something to show for it? Wealth and holiness. Wealth beyond measure, not just your own boundaries.*

WORD STUDY: THE WORD "REPENT" IS FROM THE WORD METAMORPHOSE!!

Rev 3:17-20 NKJV
Because you say, 'I am rich, have become wealthy, and have need of nothing' — and do not know that you are wretched, miserable, poor, blind, and naked — 18 I counsel you to buy from Me gold refined in the fire, that you may be rich; and white garments, that you may be clothed, that the shame of your nakedness may not be revealed; and anoint your eyes with eye salve, that you may see. 19 As many as I love, I rebuke and chasten. Therefore be zealous and repent.

REPENT
metanoeo

47

NT:3340 metanoeo (met-an-o-eh'-o); from NT:3326 and NT:3539; to think differently or afterwards, i.e. reconsider (morally, feel compunction):
KJV - repent.

REPENT IS FROM THE WORD METAMORPHOSE

metanoeo
NT:3339 metamorphoo (met-am-or-fo'-o); from NT:3326 and NT:3445; to transform (literally or figuratively, "metamorphose"):

KJV - change, transfigure, transform.

Matthew 17:2 NKJV
And was transfigured {3339} before them: and his face did shine as the sun, and his raiment was white as the light.

Mark 9:2 NKJV
And after six days Jesus taketh with him Peter, and James, and John, and leadeth them up into an high mountain apart by themselves: and he was transfigured {3339} before them.

Romans 12:2 NKJV
And be not conformed to this world: but be ye transformed {3339} by the renewing of your mind, that ye may prove what is that good, and acceptable, and perfect, will of God.

2 Corinthians 3:18 NKJV
But we all, with open face beholding as in a glass the glory of the Lord, are changed {3339} into the same image from glory to glory, even as by the Spirit of the Lord.

WORD TO PONDER: YOUR CHANGE WILL RESTORE MY POWER 3/14/08

All across the earth people are asking where is My miraculous power in the church? I AM here dear ones, to restore what has been lost. How? It is through repentance. Repentance is a change that transforms you to think differently about the positive and negative promises in My Word and how that directly applies to your life. As you see this truth it will teach you to fear Me and the power of My Word in sowing and reaping. Precious ones, it is all very clear if you would simply obey.

I AM here to restore you into alignment and obedience with My Word. I AM here to wash all the defilement from your life. I AM drawing your soul to be purged. I AM washing your defiled conscience. I AM applying fuller's soap to your thought life. I AM flushing your emotions. As you willingly offer to Me what does not align with scripture, I wash you with My blood and cover your nakedness from sin. As you heed My Word and change your ways, I wash the spots and filth and bring you through divine transformation where My image is a pure reflection in your life.

My transforming power to change is through refining fires. I AM drawing all the dross to the surface through My refiner's fire. I will open your eyes to see the dross and give you grace to surrender it to Me. True wealth is gold purchased through the great cost of going through My refiner's fire. The wealth of My power comes from learning obedience to My Word through a holy walk. The fruit of genuine repentance is change and My response to your change is the restoration of My power in your midst.

Deut 4:24 NKJV
For the LORD your God is a consuming fire, a jealous God.

Mal 3:2-3 NKJV
And who can stand when He appears? For He is like a refiner's fire and like launderers' soap. He will sit as a refiner and a purifier of silver; He will purify the sons of Levi, and purge them as gold and silver, that they may offer to the LORD an offering in righteousness.

Rev 3:3-6 NKJV
Remember therefore how you have received and heard; hold fast and repent. Therefore if you will not watch, I will come upon you as a thief, and you will not know what hour I will come upon you. 4 You have a few names even in Sardis who have not defiled their garments; and they shall walk with Me in white , for they are worthy. 5 He who overcomes shall be clothed in white garments, and I will not blot out his name from the Book of Life; but I will confess his name before My Father and before His angels. 6 "He who has an ear, let him hear what the Spirit says to the churches."'

Rev 7:14-17 NKJV
And I said to him, "Sir, you know." So he said to me, "These are the ones who come out of the great tribulation, and washed their robes and made them white in the blood of the Lamb. 15 Therefore they are before the throne of God, and serve Him day and night in His temple. And He who sits on the throne will dwell among them. 16 They shall neither hunger anymore nor thirst anymore; the sun shall not strike them, nor any heat; 17 for the Lamb who is in the midst of the throne will shepherd them and lead them to living fountains of waters. And God will wipe away every tear from their eyes."

1 Cor 6:9-11 NKJV
Do you not know that the unrighteous will not inherit the kingdom of God? Do not be deceived. Neither fornicators, nor idolaters, nor adulterers, nor homosexuals, nor sodomites, 10 nor thieves, nor covetous, nor drunkards, nor revilers, nor extortioners will inherit the kingdom of God. 11 And such were some of you. But you were washed , but you were sanctified, but you were justified in the name of the Lord Jesus and by the Spirit of our God.

Rev 19:13-14 NKJV
He was clothed with a robe dipped in blood, and His name is called The Word of God. And the armies in heaven, clothed in fine linen, white and clean, followed Him on white horses.

GODLY SORROW PRODUCES REPENTANCE/ CHANGE

RHEMA 5/13/07 GODLY SORROW

HEARD: *What's wrong with me? Underneath all the masks. Godly sorrow.*

COMMENTS: I understand godly sorrow to be the ground of repentance. I believe that this is a foretaste of circumcision and what His people will be going through when true repentance hits them. They will see and understand for the first time what disobedience costs.

2 Cor 7:9-11 NKJV
Now I rejoice, not that you were made sorry, but that your sorrow led to repentance. For you were made sorry in a godly manner, that you might suffer loss from us in nothing. For godly sorrow produces repentance leading to salvation, not to be regretted; but the sorrow of the world produces death.

2 Cor 7:8-11 AMP
For even though I did grieve you with my letter, I do not regret [it now], though I did regret it; for I see that that letter did pain you, though only for a little while; 9 Yet I am glad now, not because you were pained, but because you were pained into repentance [and so turned back to God]; for you felt a grief such as God meant you to feel, so that in nothing you might suffer loss through us or harm for what we did. 10 For godly grief and the pain God is permitted to direct, produce a repentance that leads and contributes to salvation and deliverance from evil, and it never brings regret; but worldly grief (the hopeless sorrow that is characteristic of the pagan world) is deadly [breeding and ending in death]. 11 For [you can look back now and] observe what this same godly sorrow has done for you and has produced in you: what eagerness and earnest care to explain and clear yourselves [of all complicity in the condoning of incest], what

indignation [at the sin], what alarm, what yearning, what zeal [to do justice to all concerned], what readiness to mete out punishment [to the offender]! At every point you have proved yourselves cleared and guiltless in the matter. [1 Cor 5.]

WORD TO PONDER: GODLY SORROW 5/19/07

There are times when in solitude, away from the world's escapes and people, that a deep sorrow rises from your heart and you dont understand it.   It is like a grief that squeezes your soul.   There is a yearning, a longing accompanying it, that draws you to Me in a bittersweet way. I know that you do not understand these feelings, but you recognize them.

Beloved, you are yoked with Me and My Spirit dwells within you. What you are feeling is the grief of My Spirit as I grieve over what has fallen in your life.   When you willingly turn your back on Me and choose to sin, it wounds Me. I see the long term ramification of how your choices ravage not only your life, but also affect many people, even the destinies of the lives you could have touched had you walked differently. You do not walk alone, but are a part of My body and intimately connected.

Sometimes negative reinforcement is the only way to gain your attention.   Sorrow and grief are not pleasant, but the memory of its taste is easily brought to mind.

I AM allowing you to feel a small portion of what I feel, so that it produces a Godly sorrow that leads you to repentance, salvation and deliverance. This sorrow will drive you to turn your life into making different choices and do what you can to make things right.

2 Cor 7:10-12 NLT
For God can use sorrow in our lives to help us turn away from sin and seek salvation. We will never regret that kind of sorrow. But sorrow without repentance is the kind that

52

results in death. Just see what this godly sorrow produced in you! Such earnestness, such concern to clear yourselves, such indignation, such alarm, such longing to see me, such zeal, and such a readiness to punish the wrongdoer. You showed that you have done everything you could to make things right.

AFTER THE CALL (ON 7/07/07)

I have earnestly been praying that the intercession and repentance that took place at The Call in Nashville, would be enough to turn our nation. The Call is led by Lou Engle to massively gather youth together to fast and pray for our nation. It is an awesome movement that has been going on for a number of years, moving from city to city.
http://www.thecall.com/

HEARD 7/08/07: *Heaven is for us, who can be against us? Test results. Mercy.*

HEARD: *Destiny. I will walk with you. You are not alone.*

Rom 8:31-39 NKJV
What then shall we say to these things? If God is for us , who can be against us? 32 He who did not spare His own Son, but delivered Him up for us all, how shall He not with Him also freely give us all things? 33 Who shall bring a charge against God's elect? It is God who justifies. 34 Who is he who condemns? It is Christ who died, and furthermore is also risen, who is even at the right hand of God, who also makes intercession for us . 35 Who shall separate us from the love of Christ? Shall tribulation, or distress, or persecution, or famine, or nakedness, or peril, or sword? 36 As it is written:"For Your sake we are killed all day long; We are accounted as sheep for the slaughter." 37 Yet in all these things we are more than conquerors through Him who loved us. 38 For I am persuaded that neither death nor life, nor angels nor principalities nor powers, nor things present nor things to come, 39 nor height nor depth, nor any other

created thing, shall be able to separate us from the love of God which is in Christ Jesus our Lord.

=======

RHEMA 7/11/07 GRACE FOR AMERICA

HEARD SONG: *America, America God shed His grace on thee.*

HEARD: *Canopy. Refreshment, your soul. Take time. Work load. Stress. Reassurance.*

Matt 11:28-30 NKJV
Come to Me, all you who labor and are heavy laden, and I will give you rest. 29 Take My yoke upon you and learn from Me, for I am gentle and lowly in heart, and you will find rest for your souls. 30 For My yoke is easy and My burden is light."

Intercession is Forgiveness

WHAT IS FORGIVENESS

WORD O'GRAM TO FORGIVE

To put away,
Omit, pass over or leave out,

Forsake, leave behind,
Overlook, lay aside,
Remit, yield up... the sin, offense, stumbling block, trespass,
        evil deed is
Gone and left behind, I wont carry it any more.
I choose to let go of what offends and fails to meet my
        expectations,
Valuing my freedom and their liberty more than

punishment...
Experiencing a new heart where angry bitterness once
reigned.

Rom 4:7-8 AMP
Blessed and happy and to be envied are those whose
iniquities are forgiven and whose sins are covered up and
completely buried. Blessed and happy and to be envied is
the person of whose sin the Lord will take no account nor
reckon it against him. {Ps 32:1,2.}

Matt 18:21-23 NKJV
Then Peter came to Him and said, "Lord, how often shall my
brother sin against me, and I forgive him? Up to seven
times?" Jesus said to him, "I do not say to you, up to seven
times, but up to seventy times seven.

FORGIVENESS IS AN INTERCESSION
Recently the Lord asked me if I wanted to bless a particular
person. Because of the circumstances, I understood that the
question was related to my judicial choices in spiritual
authority and my choice of being a canopy, protection and
blessing over someone as an intercessor. To be an
intercessor is a volunteer position, to lay one's life down and
serve. The job sounds heroic but is rarely pristine and
glorified on earth.

John 10:18 NLT
No one can take my life from me. I lay down my life
voluntarily. For I have the right to lay it down when I want to
and also the power to take it again. For my Father has given
me this command.

I decided to do a thorough study on what the scripture
promises us about forgiveness and intercession. I found
several surprises about what it really means to forgive, the
choices we make to remit or retain sins as intercessors and
the difference when we are personally offended.

TEACHING: UNDERSTANDING FORGIVENESS

UNDERSTANDING OLD TESTAMENT FORGIVENESS

In the OT the Hebrew word for forgiveness meant to carry or lift up and bear the offenses upon their own shoulders. They took the weight upon their own selves in lui of another carrying weight or penalty of such. It was the very act of being a mediator, intercessor or someone who was willing to bear the burden and stand in the gap or breach of sin. I found it interesting that they used the same Hebrew word when lifting up and carrying the ark upon their shoulders.

=========

Ex 32:32 NKJV
Yet now, if thou wilt forgive {5375} their sin; and if not, blot me, I pray thee, out of thy book which thou hast written.

Gen 4:13 NKJV
And Cain said unto the LORD, My punishment is greater than I can bear. {5375}

Gen 50:16-21 NKJV
'Thus you shall say to Joseph: "I beg you, please forgive {5375} the trespass of your brothers and their sin; for they did evil to you."' Now, please, forgive {5375} the trespass of the servants of the God of your father." And Joseph wept when they spoke to him. 18 Then his brothers also went and fell down before his face, and they said, "Behold, we are your servants." 19 Joseph said to them, "Do not be afraid, for am I in the place of God? 20 But as for you, you meant evil against me; but God meant it for good, in order to bring it about as it is this day, to save many people alive. 21 Now therefore, do not be afraid; I will provide for you and your little ones." And he comforted them and spoke kindly to them.

Deut 1:8-12 NKJV

Behold, I have set the land before you: go in and possess the land which the LORD sware unto your fathers, Abraham, Isaac, and Jacob, to give unto them and to their seed after them. 9 And I spake unto you at that time, saying, I am not able to bear {5375} you myself alone: 10 The LORD your God hath multiplied you, and, behold, ye are this day as the stars of heaven for multitude. 11(The LORD God of your fathers make you a thousand times so many more as ye are, and bless you, as he hath promised you!) 12 How can I myself alone bear {5375} your cumbrance, and your burden, and your strife?

Josh 3:15-17 NKJV
And as they that bare {5375} the ark were come unto Jordan, and the feet of the priests that bare {5375} the ark were dipped in the brim of the water, (for Jordan overfloweth all his banks all the time of harvest,) 16 That the waters which came down from above stood and rose up upon an heap very far from the city Adam, that is beside Zaretan: and those that came down toward the sea of the plain, even the salt sea, failed, and were cut off: and the people passed over right against Jericho. 17 And the priests that bare the ark of the covenant of the LORD stood firm on dry ground in the midst of Jordan, and all the Israelites passed over on dry ground, until all the people were passed clean over Jordan.

HEBREW TO FORGIVE

OT:5375 – To lift up and carry

OT:5375 nasa' (naw-saw'); or nacah (Ps 4:6 {OT:7}) (naw-saw'); a primitive root; to lift, in a great variety of applications, literal and figurative, absol. and rel. (as follows):

KJV - accept, advance, arise, (able to, {armor}, suffer to) bear (-er, up), bring (forth), burn, carry (away), cast, contain, desire, ease, exact, exalt (self), extol, fetch, forgive, furnish, further, give, go on, help, high, hold up, honorable (+man), lade, lay, lift (self) up, lofty, marry, magnify, needs, obtain, pardon, raise (up), receive, regard, respect, set (up), spare, stir up, swear, take (away, up), utterly, wear, yield. {quote}

AS AN INTERCESSOR, JESUS BORE OUR SINS

He lifted our sins upon Himself.

Isaiah 53 NKJV
Who has believed our report? And to whom has the arm of the LORD been revealed? 2 For He shall grow up before Him as a tender plant, And as a root out of dry ground.\He has no form or comeliness; And when we see Him, There is no beauty that we should desire Him. 3 He is despised and rejected by men, A Man of sorrows and acquainted with grief. And we hid, as it were, our faces from Him;He was despised, and we did not esteem Him.

4 Surely He has borne {#5375} our griefs and carried our sorrows; Yet we esteemed Him stricken, Smitten by God, and afflicted. 5 But He was wounded for our transgressions, He was bruised for our iniquities; The chastisement for our peace was upon Him, and by His stripes we are healed. 6 All we like sheep have gone astray; We have turned, every one, to his own way; And the LORD has laid on Him the iniquity of us all. 7 He was oppressed and He was afflicted, yet He opened not His mouth; He was led as a lamb to the slaughter, And as a sheep before its shearers is silent, so He opened not His mouth. 8 He was taken from prison and from judgment, And who will declare His generation? For He was cut off from the land of the living; For the transgressions of My people He was stricken. 9 And they made His grave with the wicked — But with the rich at His death, because He had done no violence, nor was any deceit in His mouth. 10 Yet it pleased the LORD to bruise Him; He has put Him to grief. When You make His soul an offering for sin, He shall see His seed, He shall prolong His days, and the pleasure of the LORD shall prosper in His hand. 11 He shall see the labor of His soul, and be satisfied. By His knowledge My righteous

Servant shall justify many, For He shall bear their iniquities.
12 Therefore I will divide Him a portion with the great, And
He shall divide the spoil with the strong, Because He poured
out His soul unto death, And He was numbered {4487} with
the transgressors, And He bore {#5375} the sin of many, and
made intercession {#6293} for the transgressors {#6586}.

NUMBERED

OT:4487

OT:4487 manah (maw-naw'); a primitive root; properly, to
weigh out; by implication, to allot or constitute officially; also
to enumerate or enroll:

KJV - appoint, count, number, prepare, set, tell.

Mark 15:25-28 NKJV
Now it was the third hour, and they crucified Him. 26 And the
inscription of His accusation was written above: THE KING
OF THE JEWS. 27 With Him they also crucified two robbers,
one on His right and the other on His left. 28 So the
Scripture was fulfilled which says, "And He was numbered
with the transgressors."

1 Peter 2:22-24 NKJV
"Who committed no sin, Nor was deceit found in His mouth";
23 who, when He was reviled, did not revile in return; when
He suffered, He did not threaten, but committed Himself to
Him who judges righteously; 24 who Himself bore our sins in
His own body on the tree, that we, having died to sins, might
live for righteousness..

TRANSGRESSORS
OT:6586

OT:6586 pasha` (paw-shah'); a primitive root {identical with
OT:6585 through the idea of expansion}; to break away
(from just authority), i.e. trespass, apostatize, quarrel:

KJV - offend, rebel, revolt, transgress (-ion, -or).

INTERCESSION
OT:6293

OT:6293 paga` (paw-gah'); a primitive root; to impinge (intrude, impose) , by accident or violence, or (figuratively) by importunity:

KJV - come (betwixt), cause to entreat, fall (upon), make intercession, intercessor, intreat, lay, light {upon}, meet (together), pray, reach, run.

WHEN WE ARE SENT AS INTERCESSORS IN THE NT WE HAVE THE POWER TO FORGIVE SINS OR NOT

Jesus was given the power to forgive sins. And when He sent the disciples out to pray for the sick, He gave them the same power. He said we can forgive sins or retain them. The choice is ours.

Mark 2:5-12 NKJV JESUS HAD POWER TO FORGIVE SINS
When Jesus saw their faith, He said to the paralytic, "Son, your sins are forgiven {863} you." 6 And some of the scribes were sitting there and reasoning in their hearts, 7 "Why does this Man speak blasphemies like this? Who can forgive {863} sins but God alone?" 8 But immediately, when Jesus perceived in His spirit that they reasoned thus within themselves, He said to them, "Why do you reason about these things in your hearts? 9 Which is easier, to say to the paralytic, 'Your sins are forgiven {863} you,' or to say, 'Arise, take up your bed and walk'? 10 But that you may know that the Son of Man has power on earth to forgive {863} sins" — He said to the paralytic, 11 "I say to you, arise, take up your bed, and go to your house." 12 Immediately he arose, took up the bed, and went out in the presence of them all, so that all were amazed and glorified God, saying, "We never saw anything like this!"

John 20:20-23 NKJV JESUS SENT THEM WITH POWER AND CHOICE TO FORGIVE

When He had said this, He showed them His hands and His side. Then the disciples were glad when they saw the Lord. 21 So Jesus said to them again, "Peace to you! As the Father has sent Me, I also send you." 22 And when He had said this, He breathed on them, and said to them, "Receive the Holy Spirit. 23 If you forgive {863} the sins of any, they are forgiven {863} them; if you retain the sins of any, they are retained."

TO FORGIVE: To let go and leave
NT:863 – To let go and leave

NT:863 aphiemi (af-ee'-ay-mee); from NT:575 and hiemi (to send; an intens. form of eimi, to go); to send forth, in various applications (as follow):

KJV - cry, forgive, forsake, lay aside, leave, let (alone, be, go, have), omit, put (send) away, remit, suffer, yield up.

TO RETAIN: To hold on and keep
Krateo – To hold on and keep

NT:2902 krateo (krat-eh'-o); from NT:2904; to use strength, i.e. seize or retain (literally or figuratively):

KJV - hold (by, fast), keep, lay hand (hold) on, obtain, retain, take (by).

Rom 4:6-8 NLT
King David spoke of this, describing the happiness of an undeserving sinner who is declared to be righteous: 7 "Oh, what joy for those whose disobedience is forgiven, whose sins are put out of sight. {863} 8 Yes, what joy for those whose sin is no longer counted against them by the Lord."

1 Cor 7:12-13 KJV
If any brother hath a wife that believeth not, and she be pleased to dwell with him, let him not put her away. {863} 13

And the woman which hath an husband that believeth not, and if he be pleased to dwell with her, let her not leave him. {863}

Rev 2:4 KJV
Nevertheless I have somewhat against thee, because thou hast left {863} thy first love.

John 12:7 KJV
Then said Jesus, Let her alone: {863} against the day of my burying hath she kept this.

HOWEVER WHEN WE ARE PERSONALLY OFFENDED, WE MUST FORGIVE UNLESS WE WANT TO BEAR THE PENALTY

1. WE ARE NOT FORGIVEN UNLESS WE FORGIVE

Mark 11:25-26 KJV
And when ye stand praying, forgive, if ye have ought against any: that your Father also which is in heaven may forgive {#863} you your trespasses. But if ye do not forgive, {#863} neither will your Father which is in heaven forgive your trespasses. {3900}

Matt 6:14-15 NKJV
"For if you forgive men their trespasses, your heavenly Father will also forgive you. 15 But if you do not forgive {#863} men their trespasses, neither will your Father forgive {#863} your trespasses.

3900 Trespasses

paraptoma
NT:3900 paraptoma (par-ap'-to-mah); from NT:3895; a side-slip (lapse or deviation), i.e. (unintentional) error or (wilful) transgression:
KJV - fall, fault, offence, sin, trespass.

2. WE RISK BEING SENT TO THE PRISON OF TORMENT IF WE DO NOT FORGIVE

Matt 18:34-35 KJV THE FATHER CAN SEND US TO BE TORMENTED
And his lord was wroth, and delivered him to the tormentors, till he should pay all that was due unto him. 35 So likewise shall my heavenly Father do also unto you, if ye from your hearts forgive {#863} not every one his brother their trespasses.

3. THE SAME MEASURE WE FORGIVE, THE SAME MEASURE WE RECEIVE FORGIVENESS

Gal 6:7-8 NKJV
Do not be deceived, God is not mocked; for whatever a man sows, that he will also reap.

Luke 6:37-38 NKJV
"Judge not, and you shall not be judged. Condemn not, and you shall not be condemned. Forgive, {#863} and you will be forgiven {#863} ... For with the same measure that you use, it will be measured back to you."

4. WE RISK NOT BEING HEALED IF WE ARE NOT FORGIVEN

{Healing and Forgiveness are connected} Remember we must forgive in order to be forgiven.

James 5:14-16 KJV
Is any sick among you? let him call for the elders of the church; and let them pray over him, anointing him with oil in the name of the Lord: 15 And the prayer of faith shall save the sick, and the Lord shall raise him up; and if he have committed sins, they shall be forgiven him. 16 Confess your faults one to another, and pray one for another, that ye may

be healed. The effectual fervent prayer of a righteous man availeth much.

Matt 9:2 NKJV
Then behold, they brought to Him a paralytic lying on a bed. When Jesus saw their faith, He said to the paralytic, "Son, be of good cheer; your sins are forgiven you."

John 5:14 NKJV
Afterward Jesus found him in the temple, and said to him, "See, you have been made well. Sin no more, lest a worse thing come upon you."

Ps 103:3 NKJV
Who forgives all your iniquities, Who heals all your diseases.

2 Chron 7:14-15 NKJV
If My people who are called by My name will humble themselves, and pray and seek My face, and turn from their wicked ways, then I will hear from heaven, and will forgive their sin and heal their land.

5. OUR ACCUSERS CAN SEND US TO PRISON IF WE ARE NOT FORGIVEN

Remember we must forgive in order to be forgiven.

Matt 5:23-26 AMP 23 So if when you are offering your gift at the altar you there remember that your brother has any {grievance} against you, 24 Leave your gift at the altar and go. First make peace with your brother, and then come back and present your gift. 25 Come to terms quickly with your accuser while you are on the way traveling with him, lest your accuser hand you over to the judge, and the judge to the guard, and you be put in prison. 26 Truly I say to you, you will not be released until you have paid the last fraction of a penny.

TO FORGIVE

Papa You told me to always forgive,
seven times seven that I might live.
For if I don't forgive others, this I see -
How can You also totally forgive Me?

It is in extending mercy that I receive back
My seeds sown from going around the track.
These endless circles have got to stop.
I know not how, until I reach the top.

On this tall mountain, this stumbling block.
My life keeps ticking going around the clock.
Faith moves mountains and sends them to sea.
Why oh why can't I heal me?

I have taken on too much to see the whole
What I need today is Your touch to my soul.
Help me to release the anger I feel
And come into alignment with Your truth that is real.

My forgiveness releases the soul that is hardened.
It allows You to work because I have pardoned.
Let not this person be tormented with hell
Rather please release and please make well.

For all of us are in need of repair
We each have faced our own despair.
I can not hold back what You freely give.
I release my judgment so that we both may live.

Matt 6:14-15 NKJV
*"For if you forgive men their trespasses, your heavenly Father will
also forgive you. But if you do not forgive men their trespasses,
neither will your Father forgive your trespasses.*

Intercession is the Sacrifice of Standing in the Gap

For several seasons the Holy Spirit has been wooing the hearts of His people and literally fulfilling the following verse: "And he will turn the hearts of the fathers to the children, and the hearts of the children to their fathers, lest I come and strike the earth with a curse." (Mal 4:6) When this massive move of the Holy Spirit began to unfold, I witnessed this turning in many ways (especially in the Promise Keepers movement) but I never understood the curse part until recently.

Now everywhere we turn, we hear the prophets speak of coming judgment. Many of us have felt so overwhelmed by the stacked deck we do not realize that we still have a vote in this matter. Scripture tells us that mercy triumphs over judgment whether it is averted totally, or reduced to a spanking. Simply put, judgment hangs in the balance and our vote still counts. At this late hour and with so much against us, how do we cast our vote and stand in the gap for the sins of our nation, our world, our children?

The gap is a breach in our hedge of protection, where the enemy is allowed to start a fire then take advantage of the course it takes. To stand against this, it requires courageous fire fighters, willing to take the heat and battle the flames. There are many ways to fight a fire and it all depends upon the tools we are given. The following story was forwarded to me this week. I believe it portrays God's answer to the greatest tool we can use, and it also sheds light on the verse, "And he will turn the hearts of the fathers to the children, and the hearts of the children to their fathers, lest I come and strike the earth with a curse." (Mal 4:6)

The author writes about reading an article in the National Geographic several years ago: "After a forest fire in Yellowstone National Park, forest rangers began their trek up a mountain to assess the inferno's damage. One ranger found a bird literally petrified in ashes, perched statuesquely on the ground at the base of a tree.

Somewhat sickened by the eerie sight, he knocked over the bird with a stick. When he struck it, three tiny chicks scurried from under their dead mother's wings. The loving mother, keenly aware of impending disaster, had carried her offspring to the base of the tree and had gathered them under her wings, instinctively knowing that the toxic smoke would rise. She could have flown to safety but had refused to abandon her babies. When the blaze had arrived and the heat had singed her small body, the mother remained steadfast. Because she had been willing to die, those under the cover of her wings would live." [author unknown]

"This is My commandment, that you love one another as I have loved you. Greater love has no one than this, than to lay down one's life for his friends." (John 15: 12,13) If you feel the heat of judgment coming your way, consider what you may do to make a difference for those under your wings. Your vote counts. How do I know? Because love still covers a multitude of sins.

~~~~~~~~~~~~

WORD STUDY ON STANDING IN THE GAP
"And I sought for a man among them, that should make up the hedge, and stand <05975> in the gap <06556> before me for the land, that I should not destroy it: but I found none. (Ezekiel 22:30 KJV)

STAND IN THE HEBREW:
05975 'amad {aw-mad'} ¤ a primitive root; TWOT - 1637; v ¤ AV - stood 171, stand 137, (raise, stand...) up 42, set 32, stay 17, still 15, appointed 10, standing 10, endure 8, remain 8, present 7, continue 6, withstand 6, waited 5, establish 5, misc 42; 521 ¤ 1) to stand, remain, endure, take one's stand 1a) (Qal) 1a1) to stand, take one's stand, be in a standing

attitude, stand forth, take a stand, present oneself, attend upon, be or become servant of 1a2) to stand still, stop (moving or doing), cease 1a3) to tarry, delay, remain, continue, abide, endure, persist, be steadfast 1a4) to make a stand, hold one's ground 1a5) to stand upright, remain standing, stand up, rise, be erect, be upright 1a6) to arise, appear, come on the scene, stand forth, appear, rise up or against 1a7) to stand with, take one's stand, be appointed, grow flat, grow insipid 1b) (Hiphil) 1b1) to station, set 1b2) to cause to stand firm, maintain 1b3) to cause to stand up, cause to set up, erect 1b4) to present (one) before (king) 1b5) to appoint, ordain, establish 1c) (Hophal) to be presented, be caused to stand, be stood before

GAP IN THE HEBREW
06556 perets {peh'-rets} ¤ from 06555; TWOT - 1826a; n m ¤ AV - breach 14, gap 2, breaking 1, breaking forth 1, breaking in 1; 19 ¤ 1) breach, gap, bursting forth 1a) bursting forth, outburst 1b) breach 1c) broken wall 1d) outburst (fig. of God's wrath)

WORD TO PONDER: STAND IN THE GAP
As Achan's sin caused the entire camp to fall, so it is when there is a breach in the hedge of protection. However, the reverse principle works as well. Through one man's favor, standing in that gap can cause safety for all those within.

If you could but believe it, I can use you to stand for those you love. Your obedience, your sacrifice, your Godly decisions, your standing against an enemy onslaught on their behalf makes all the difference to their safety. I need someone who is willing to stand in the breaches along the hedge to help form a solid protection around those you love. Will you consider standing for their sake? Do understand the breach is where the enemy rushes in, so you must be willing to stand against such. Yet I give the grace and power to those I call to do so. And if these loved ones belong to you, I have already given you the authority.

"And I sought for a man among them, that should make up the hedge, and stand in the gap before me for the land, that I should not destroy it: but I found none." (Ezekiel 22:30 KJV)

KEEPING THE CHILDREN

RHEMA 5/18/07 KEEP THE CHILDREN

HEARD: *The war outside.*

HEARD: *I went through the world and sought for a man to stand in the gap. One who has no personal agenda. One who is willing to make a difference. One who understands the process.*

{Lord to stand in the gap for what particular issue?}

HEARD: *My children. Count them one by one. The ones who know Me and stay aligned. Graft them in.*

Exactly. Before you met me, I was an outcast. Now I am no longer alone. That I might have life. That you might have life. Abundantly.

PIX: *I saw that I had in my hands a string of gems that was twirling and twisting. It looked like a fine necklace.*

Isa 54:11-14 NKJV
"O you afflicted one, Tossed with tempest, and not comforted, Behold, I will lay your stones with colorful gems, And lay your foundations with sapphires. 12 I will make your pinnacles of rubies, Your gates of crystal, And all your walls of precious stones. 13 All your children shall be taught by the LORD, And great shall be the peace of your children . 14 In righteousness you shall be established; You shall be far from

oppression, for you shall not fear; And from terror, for it shall not come near you.

Wait {Hebrew} To bring together by twisting

qavah
OT:6960 qavah (kaw-vaw'); a primitive root; to bind together (perhaps by twisting), i.e. collect; (figuratively) to expect: KJV - gather (together), look, patiently, tarry, wait (for, on, upon).

(Biblesoft's New Exhaustive Strong's Numbers and Concordance with Expanded Greek-Hebrew Dictionary. Copyright © 1994, 2003 Biblesoft, Inc. and International Bible Translators, Inc.)

Isa 49:22-23 NKJV
Thus says the Lord GOD: "Behold, I will lift My hand in an oath to the nations, And set up My standard for the peoples; They shall bring your sons in their arms, And your daughters shall be carried on their shoulders; 23 Kings shall be your foster fathers, And their queens your nursing mothers; They shall bow down to you with their faces to the earth, And lick up the dust of your feet. Then you will know that I am the LORD, For they shall not be ashamed who wait {6960} for Me."

PIX: *I saw something written on the black board. It was the word, "WHY" And it was underlined to bring emphasis.*

HEARD: *The world goes through its storm. Noah's ark. Night resurrection. Redeemed, welcome. Sent to occupy. Worn in two. This land is very ours. Liberate.*

DREAM: *I prophesied to the president of the US and said that we need to turn around and go the right way. I said and it is not about us, it's about our children.*

2 Chron 16:9 NKJV

For the eyes of the LORD run to and fro throughout the whole earth, to show Himself strong on behalf of those whose heart is loyal to Him.

Ezek 22:29-31 NKJV
So I sought for a man among them who would make a wall, and stand in the gap before Me on behalf of the land, that I should not destroy it; but I found no one. 31 Therefore I have poured out My indignation on them; I have consumed them with the fire of My wrath; and I have recompensed their deeds on their own heads," says the Lord GOD.

2 Chron 6:19-20 NKJV
Yet regard the prayer of Your servant and his supplication, O LORD my God, and listen to the cry and the prayer which Your servant is praying before You: 20 that Your eyes may be open toward this temple day and night, toward the place where You said You would put Your name, that You may hear the prayer which Your servant makes toward this place.

Ps 34:15-17 NKJV
The eyes of the LORD are on the righteous, And His ears are open to their cry. 16 The face of the LORD is against those who do evil, To cut off the remembrance of them from the earth. 17 The righteous cry out, and the LORD hears, And delivers them out of all their troubles.

Prov 15:3 NKJV
The eyes of the LORD are in every place, Keeping watch on the evil and the good.

Jer 32:19-20 NKJV
You are great in counsel and mighty in work, for your eyes are open to all the ways of the sons of men, to give everyone according to his ways and according to the fruit of his doings.

QUICKENED REOCCURRING SONG: *I surrender all.*

HEARD 10/03/07: *Storm. Whether you know it or not. Soul surgery. To find the answers. My goodness will help you through it.*

PIX: *I saw a piece of paper like an email that was from an Intercessor.*

HEARD: *I am confirming your place.*

VISION: *I saw a huge face of a man in the moving clouds.*

{Lord who was that?}

HEARD: *A Watcher.*

HEARD: *About face. What difference does it make? Your calling. An entire generation kept. Stay and dont leave us. Excellent. We will fight with you. Your hosts. To keep them from being plundered. Diamonds, your jewels, your babies.*

WORD TO PONDER: YOUR ABIDING MATTERS TO YOUR CHILDREN 10/03/07

Beloved parents, because I have heard your prayers over your loved ones, I AM fulfilling My part to help you stay obedient. It is My goodness that takes you through personal storms, to excise the rebellion and disobedience out of your walk, so that the bad seeds and fruit will not be passed down to your children. Yes chastening and surgery does hurt. But My discipline produces the fruit of rightful living whereby you are conformed to My will and purpose in your thoughts and actions.

Your obedience to follow My Word and your conscience is an intercession that covers and keeps your children from being plundered. Stay with them, abide with them by being faithful to Me. This is a part of your spiritual authority, a canopy where your choices matter and make a difference. As you obey, the angelic hosts fight with you to keep your babies. Vast are your babies. Even generations not yet born are your progeny. For your sake, I will remember your faithful walk and prayers and pass the fruit of such down to your progeny. When you are tempted to stray away, remember your children and walk in love by knowing your fruits of obedience. Great shall be the peace of your children and they shall be established in righteousness.

Isa 54:8-17 NKJV
With a little wrath I hid My face from you for a moment; But with everlasting kindness I will have mercy on you, "Says the LORD, your Redeemer. 9 "For this is like the waters of Noah to Me; For as I have sworn That the waters of Noah would no longer cover the earth, So have I sworn That I would not be angry with you, nor rebuke you. 10 For the mountains shall depart And the hills be removed, But My kindness shall not depart from you,Nor shall My covenant of peace be removed, "Says the LORD, who has mercy on you. 11 "O you afflicted one, Tossed with tempest, and not comforted, Behold, I will lay your stones with colorful gems, And lay your foundations with sapphires. 12 I will make your pinnacles of rubies, Your gates of crystal, And all your walls of precious stones. 13 All your children shall be taught by the LORD, And great shall be the peace of your children . 14 In righteousness you shall be established; You shall be far from oppression, for you shall not fear; And from terror, for it shall not come near you. 15 Indeed they shall surely assemble, but not because of Me. Whoever assembles against you shall fall for your sake. 16 "Behold, I have created the blacksmith Who blows the coals in the fire, Who brings forth an instrument for his work; And I have created the spoiler to destroy. 17 No weapon formed against you shall prosper, And every tongue which rises against you in judgment You shall condemn. This is the heritage of the servants of the LORD, And their righteousness is from Me, "Says the LORD.

Heb 12:10-11 AMP

For [our earthly fathers] disciplined us for only a short period of time and chastised us as seemed proper and good to them; but He disciplines us for our certain good, that we may become sharers in His own holiness. For the time being no discipline brings joy, but seems grievous and painful; but afterwards it yields a peaceable fruit of righteousness to those who have been trained by it [a harvest of fruit which consists in righteousness — in conformity to God's will in purpose, thought, and action, resulting in right living and right standing with God].

Ex 20:5-6 NKJV
For I, the LORD your God, am a jealous God, visiting the iniquity of the fathers upon the children to the third and fourth generations of those who hate Me, but showing mercy to thousands, to those who love Me and keep My commandments.

Deut 7:9-10 NKJV
"Therefore know that the LORD your God, He is God, the faithful God who keeps covenant and mercy for a thousand generations with those who love Him and keep His commandments.

TO PARTNER WITH HIM IN PRAYER

From the passion of Your bosom,
I feel the heartbeats of Your love.
How you continue to incubate,
I know not how or of.

But Your Words just keep on flowing
With understanding and knowing.
They pour out upon the earth -
Your giant womb yet to give birth.

The times and seasons are in Your great hands.
It's not in the agenda or hands of man.
In the fullness of time, ripe, they burst forth.

Carried forth by angels on wings that soar.

Each Word is nurtured and coddled with care,
With men and angels united so rare.
Spanning Your bridge as from heaven to earth,
Each Word is a jewel, destined with worth.

Let Your will be done on earth as in heaven,
Your grace is sufficient to take out leaven.
To guard and to keep what is absolute Thine
Kept pure and holy even as it's refined.

Please impart us this day our daily bread
Let Your manna fall that we may be fed.
We sup at Your table drinking Your cup,
We lean into You to hear what is up.

Grant us ears to hear and grant eyes to see
That we may partner, uniting with Thee.
As we labor to enter with trust and belief
Grant understanding, providing relief.

We desire to please You with our effort,
God forbid that what we carry might abort.
We are weak at most and ignorant at best
To know how to nurture and guard our own nest.

We wait upon You to train us to defend.
Our backs are together looking out and in.
To protect from marauder's attempt to fear.
And to see the young incubating so near.

Yes birds of a feather do flock together,
Waiting for loved ones whose feet are still tethered.
Given tasks to perform while we are waiting,
While the demonic floods are still abating.

The earth is drying from our time in Your ark,
With anticipation we're waiting to embark.
Not in, but out, Your door of eminent hope,

Promised to the prophets, as seen through their scope.

We'll come out Your door with families intact
Prepared to gather anything we lack.
The slates wiped clean with pure new beginnings,
From disciplined lives, repentant from sinning.

Jesus' blood and grace is more than enough
To keep us from stumbling from rocks too rough.
We hold the hands of the weak and feeble,
Bringing them along making sure they're able.

Bravely taking the journey to our new land,
United, moving on, and making our stand.
What a joy to witness our promised new place
Prosperous and healthy, poured from Your grace.

So as we wait by our nest in Your vast love,
We will rest in Your hope and plan from above.
That our loved ones are incubating, safe and sound
As we declare Your great Words, that they may abound.

Hos 2:14-16 NLT
"But then I will win her back once again. I will lead her out into
the desert and speak tenderly to her there. I will return her
vineyards to her and transform the Valley of Trouble into gateway
of hope. She will give herself to me there, as she did long ago when
she was young, when I freed her from her captivity in Egypt. "In
that coming day," says the LORD, "you will call me 'my husband'
instead of 'my master.'

HOLDING ONTO YOUR LOVED ONES

HEARD 6/05/07: *Crossing over. In the next days, all accomplished. Zeal for My house, you have done well. All present and accounted for.*

PIX: *I saw some salt that had been placed on my grandson's lips and he was tasting it.*

76

[Salt is a keeping preservative.]

KEEPING YOUR LOVED ONES IS SCRIPTURAL

- All That Sailed With Paul On His Ship

Acts 27:22-24 NKJV
And now I urge you to take heart, for there will be no loss of life among you, but only of the ship. For there stood by me this night an angel of the God to whom I belong and whom I serve, saying, 'Do not be afraid, Paul; you must be brought before Caesar; and indeed God has granted you all those who sail with you.'

- All That Were In The Same House Under The Blood

Ex 12:22-24 NKJV
And you shall take a bunch of hyssop, dip it in the blood that is in the basin, and strike the lintel and the two doorposts with the blood that is in the basin. And none of you shall go out of the door of his house until morning. 23 For the LORD will pass through to strike the Egyptians; and when He sees the blood on the lintel and on the two doorposts, the LORD will pass over the door and not allow the destroyer to come into your houses to strike you.

- Noah's Family And All That Were In The Ark

Gen 7:13-16 NKJV
On the very same day Noah and Noah's sons, Shem, Ham, and Japheth, and Noah's wife and the three wives of his sons with them, entered the ark — 14 they and every beast after its kind, all cattle after their kind, every creeping thing that creeps on the earth after its kind, and every bird after its kind, every bird of every sort. 15 And they went into the ark to Noah , two by two, of all flesh in which is the breath of life. 16 So those that entered, male and female of all flesh, went in as God had commanded him; and the LORD shut him in.

- Rahab's Request That Her Family Is Spared

Josh 2:18-19 NKJV
When we come into the land, you bind this line of scarlet cord in the window through which you let us down, and unless you bring your father, your mother, your brothers, and all your father's household to your own home. 19 So it shall be that whoever goes outside the doors of your house into the street, his blood shall be on his own head, and we will be guiltless.

- Lot Is Safe Because Of Abraham's Prayers

Gen 19:29 NKJV
And it came to pass, when God destroyed the cities of the plain, that God remembered Abraham , and sent Lot out of the midst of the overthrow, when He overthrew the cities in which Lot had dwelt.

Gen 18:16-28 NKJV
Then the men rose from there and looked toward Sodom, and Abraham went with them to send them on the way. 17 And the LORD said, "Shall I hide from Abraham what I am doing, 18 since Abraham shall surely become a great and mighty nation, and all the nations of the earth shall be blessed in him? 19 For I have known him, in order that he may command his children and his household after him, that they keep the way of the LORD, to do righteousness and justice, that the LORD may bring to Abraham what He has spoken to him." 20 And the LORD said, "Because the outcry against Sodom and Gomorrah is great, and because their sin is very grave, 21 I will go down now and see whether they have done altogether according to the outcry against it that has come to Me; and if not, I will know." 22 Then the men turned away from there and went toward Sodom, but Abraham still stood before the LORD. 23 And Abraham came near and said,"Would You also destroy the righteous with the wicked? 24 Suppose there were fifty righteous within the city; would You also destroy the place and not spare it for the fifty righteous that were in it? 25 Far be it

from You to do such a thing as this, to slay the righteous with the wicked, so that the righteous should be as the wicked; far be it from You! Shall not the Judge of all the earth do right?" 26 So the LORD said,"If I find in Sodom fifty righteous within the city, then I will spare all the place for their sakes." 27 Then Abraham answered and said, "Indeed now, I who am but dust and ashes have taken it upon myself to speak to the Lord: 28 Suppose there were five less than the fifty righteous; would You destroy all of the city for lack of five?

- Cities of Refuge Appointed

Num 35:6-7 NKJV
"Now among the cities which you will give to the Levites you shall appoint six cities of refuge, to which a manslayer may flee. And to these you shall add forty-two cities .

- Joseph Saves His Family From the Great Famine

Gen 47:1 NKJV
Then Joseph went and told Pharaoh, and said, "My father and my brothers, their flocks and their herds and all that they possess, have come from the land of Canaan; and indeed they are in the land of Goshen.

- The Unbelieving is Set Apart When Living with the Believer

1 Cor 7:12-16 NKJV
But to the rest I, not the Lord, say: If any brother has a wife who does not believe, and she is willing to live with him, let him not divorce her. 13 And a woman who has a husband who does not believe, if he is willing to live with her, let her not divorce him. 14 For the unbelieving husband is sanctified by the wife, and the unbelieving wife is sanctified by the husband; otherwise your children would be unclean, but now they are holy. 15 But if the unbeliever departs, let him depart; a brother or a sister is not under bondage in such cases. But God has called us to peace. 16 For how do you

know, O wife, whether you will save your husband? Or how do you know, O husband, whether you will save your wife?

WARNING FROM WISDOM: When I was praying over this, the Lord emphasized the following scripture to me:

Acts 27:24; 32 NKJV
"...indeed God has granted you all those who sail with you.' ... Paul said to the centurion and the soldiers, **"Unless these men stay in the ship, you cannot be saved."**

It is very important that in keeping your loved ones, that you do not cut off relationship with them. Remain loving, forgiving, supportive in intercessory prayer. If they have forsaken your loving covering and broken relationship with you, and you have tried to repair it without success, release them to the Lord as the father did over his prodigal son. {Luke 15}

The Lord will deal with them in the world of famine until they come to their right senses and return in humble repentance. After much intercession over the prodigals, the Lord has convinced me that famine, not coddling is the only way to draw them home again. He grants all people free will and as intercessors, we too must honor the free wills of those who depart. Always look for and expect their return, just as the father did and warmly welcome the prodigal with open arms, open heart and without condemnation, accusation and judgment. Great joy will take place in that day!

Luke 15:13-24 NKJV
And not many days after, the younger son gathered all together, journeyed to a far country, and there wasted his possessions with prodigal living. 14 But when he had spent all, there arose a severe famine in that land, and he began to be in want. 15 Then he went and joined himself to a citizen of that country, and he sent him into his fields to feed swine.

16 And he would gladly have filled his stomach with the pods that the swine ate, and no one gave him anything. 17 "But when he came to himself, he said, 'How many of my father's hired servants have bread enough and to spare, and I perish with hunger! 18 I will arise and go to my father, and will say to him, "Father, I have sinned against heaven and before you, 19 and I am no longer worthy to be called your son. Make me like one of your hired servants."'

"And he arose and came to his father. But when he was still a great way off, his father saw him and had compassion, and ran and fell on his neck and kissed him. 21 And the son said to him, 'Father, I have sinned against heaven and in your sight, and am no longer worthy to be called your son.'

"But the father said to his servants, 'Bring out the best robe and put it on him, and put a ring on his hand and sandals on his feet. 23 And bring the fatted calf here and kill it, and let us eat and be merry; 24 for this my son was dead and is alive again; he was lost and is found.' And they began to be merry.

Amos 8:11-12 NKJV
"Behold, the days are coming," says the Lord GOD, "That I will send a famine on the land, Not a famine of bread, Nor a thirst for water, But of hearing the words of the LORD. 12 They shall wander from sea to sea, And from north to east; They shall run to and fro, seeking the word of the LORD, But shall not find it.

Isa 60:5 NKJV
Arise, shine; For your light has come! And the glory of the LORD is risen upon you. 2 For behold, the darkness shall cover the earth, and deep darkness the people; But the LORD will arise over you, And His glory will be seen upon you. 3 The Gentiles shall come to your light, And kings to the brightness of your rising. 4 "Lift up your eyes all around, and see: They all gather together, they come to you; Your sons shall come from afar, And your daughters shall be nursed at your side. 5 Then you shall see and become radiant, And

your heart shall swell with joy; Because the abundance of the sea shall be turned to you, The wealth of the Gentiles shall come to you.

RESCUE OUR PRODIGALS

Lord, so many are crying for lost loved ones,
Who are lost in the world of prodigal sons.
Let the tears that fall, having spent all our words,
Be powerful prayers for what has gone absurd.

With hearts that are torn and sometimes without hope
We yearn over our children and ask for more rope.
To rescue the wild ones, those who buck and kick
Send forth your lassoing angels to draw them back.

Let them hunger and thirst for the Words from heaven
Forsaking their sin, and lives filled with leaven.
Draw them to return, to Your truth that they know.
Do all it takes to rescue them in tow.

Luke 15:14,15, 17 NKJV
But when he had spent all, there arose a severe famine in that land, and he began to be in want... "But when he came to himself, he said, 'How many of my father's hired servants have bread enough and to spare, and I perish with hunger!

TO STAND FOR A FRIEND

By Wayne Warner... and a note from Sandy

Attending a conference, recently I watched a drama in real life play out in front of me. I watched a fellow go up for prayer and stand a very long time waiting for the speaker to pray for him. He had driven from out of town and especially wanted prayer. Every time the speaker would get close, he would zig zag the other direction and miss this hopeful man.

This happened numerous times and finally I could tell that the speaker was about to leave without praying for him.

At that realization I overheard our pastor's wife say, "I am going up front to get prayer for my friend." As she moved up to the front, I saw Sandy and the man's wife stand up elsewhere and move forward with the same intention. I talked with them later and they all knew the speaker was about to leave without praying for this man. The Holy Spirit birthed in their hearts to be a mediator.

They gathered around the man and the speaker — and sure enough, as the speaker turned around, he turned the other direction and missed the man. Sandy was the only person left actually facing the speaker and she grabbed his hand as he was moving towards the door. "This man needs your prayers," she said as she placed the speaker's hand upon the man's heart. You could tell the speaker was surprised! He immediately began to pray for this man with his three friends standing with them and agreeing in prayer.

[Note from Sandy - It was incredible that I actually had the courage to do that! However I was driven by love and the urgency of intercession. From a different place in the auditorium I watched the same drama play out and the Lord so touched me with the pain of dashed hopes. I was in agony feeling the pull and tug of my friend's heart as the speaker got near, then moved away — over and over again.] [End of Sandy note]

What was quickened to me as I watched this whole drama play out was the story in Mark 2 about the paralyzed man and his friends. Four men carried a paralyzed man to Jesus on a stretcher, that he might be healed. When they realized they could not find a way to Jesus through the crowds or through a blocked door, they searched for another way. They saw a possibility through the roof and set about acquiring ropes and ladders. It must have been difficult to hoist the paralyzed man up onto the roof, but they were determined to get him to Jesus. Once they were on the roof, they faced the task of opening a hole that was big enough to lower the paralyzed man's stretcher down in front of Jesus.

I can imagine the turmoil that these friends caused by digging a hole in the roof above Jesus and the crowds. Can't you just hear all the grumbling as they went about their task? "Hey you're making too much noise." "What a mess!" "Stop interrupting the meeting!" But these friends would not be stopped. Working together, finally after a tiring and laborious process they lowered the paralyzed man down in front of Jesus.

It is interesting that Jesus always goes right to the source of the trouble. These friends wanted this man to be healed. But Jesus probably surprised them by forgiving his sins. After all the work they had gone to and Jesus forgives his sins? But the Lord is in the business of healing the whole man, both the body and the soul. These friends got even more from Jesus than they had hoped for. Their friend was both healed and forgiven — what a gift.

After witnessing the drama at the conference and then thinking about this section of scripture, the Lord opened my mind to see that in most cases a person who is suffering and afflicted needs real friends to place them at the feet of our Lord Jesus. In the case of the paralyzed man, his friends had to be in one accord. First they had to agree that their friend's need was something they could not meet. Second, these friends had to agree that they believed Jesus could meet the need. Third, these friends had to agree to a plan to get their friend to Jesus. Fourth, these friends had to work together to make their plan work. Fifth, these friends had to agree that nothing would stop them from getting their friend to Jesus.

I believe that what the church needs today are more friends that will go the distance for a friend in need. They need to be willing to overcome fear of man's opinions, be persistent, and be willing to be held responsible for any mess that accrues in reaching Jesus.

"Greater love has no one than this, than to lay down one's life for his friends." (John 15:13 NKJV)

Lovingly,
Wayne & Sandy Warner

STANDING IN THE GAP FOR OUR TROOPS

Declaration Over Those Who Are Our Children In The Spirit {adapted from Psalms 91}

Our sons and daughters who are in the middle east (and all around the world) walk forth under the shelter of the Most High and find rest under the shadow of the Almighty.

This we declare of the LORD: because He alone is our refuge, our place of safety; He is our God, and we are trusting Him.

For He will rescue our children from every trap and protect them from the fatal plague.

He will shield them with His wings. He will shelter our children with His feathers. His faithful promises are their armor and protection.

Our faithful warriors will not be afraid of the terrors of the night, nor fear the dangers of the day,

Nor will they dread the plague that stalks in darkness, nor the disaster that strikes at midday.

Though the death angel is near their side, these evils will not touch our children.

They will see it with their own eyes; they will see how the wicked are punished.

Because we their parents have made the LORD our refuge, and do make the Most High our shelter,

No evil will conquer them; no plague will come near their dwelling.

For He orders His angels to protect them wherever they go.

They will hold our children with their hands to keep them from stumbling.

Our sons and daughters will trample down lions and poisonous snakes; they will crush fierce lions and serpents under their feet!

The LORD says, "I will rescue those who are not innocent, because you love Me. I will protect your children because you trust in My name.

When you call on Me, I will answer; I will be with your children in trouble. I will rescue them and honor them.

I will satisfy them with a long life and give them My salvation."

STANDING IN THE BREACH OF THE "FAULT" LINE

TRANCE VISION 7/01/01: *I had done some kind of a search in the data base and I saw each of the states in the USA scrolling past me. Suddenly I was standing on a fault line on the earth and I had one foot on each side and I was praying,* *knowing I needed to choose which side to stand on because the earth was splitting underneath my feet.*

HEARD: *America. Speechless.*

PIX: *I saw a camera mounted on a ceiling and it was scanning the view. I saw my finger pointing the same direction that the camera was spanning.*

HEARD: *Delighted to help. Grounded in prayer. Subjected by time and space.*

EXPERIENCE: Last night I traveled out of town and was visiting a prayer meeting. When I came into the sanctuary my eye glanced at the 2 banners at the front: Restore the foundations and Rebuilding the Ruins and being the Repairers of the Breach. It was impressed upon me that these 2 Words were a commission of destiny.

Later when I mentioned the 2 banners and the commission to one of the intercessors, she mentioned each banner was made for a conference and that the last banner for their last conference was never made. I jumped on that and said, "What is the banner??? It is a prophetic Word!" I knew that whatever the title was, it had not yet been fulfilled because of the parable that she had not yet made the banner. She said it was the Coming of His Glory.

During worship today I was looking at the crack in the concrete and thinking how it reminded me of the vision I had last night about standing on each side of the fault line. Later the pastor shared how important it is to forgive. My eye glanced and I was amazed as he stood with one foot on either side of the split of concrete running down the center of the church, and his feet were also standing on the crack line just as he said that. Then when the youth leader shared about 7/07/07, she too stood on the same crack at that moment and then stepped off.

The Word the Lord downloaded into my spirit was that as we stood in the breach of the "fault" lines and forgive offenses, it would be multiplied for God's glory to return.

Ezek 22:30-31 NKJV
So I sought for a man among them who would make a wall, and stand in the gap before Me on behalf of the land, that I should not destroy it; but I found no one. 31 Therefore I have poured out My indignation on them; I have consumed them with the fire of My wrath; and I have recompensed their deeds on their own heads," says the Lord GOD.

WORD TO PONDER: TO DELIVER THE UNRIGHTEOUS 11/9/00

By their fruits you shall know them. This is true in every walk of life, including cites. Use this knowledge for prayer. It is in the evil fruits of each city that you will know their strongholds and high places. I will reveal to you the works within your city walls, and you shall be able to identify the evil rulers that empower such unrighteousness.

As you are willing to stand against the evil, and pray forgiveness for the sins of the people, I AM willing to use you as an intercessor to stand in the gap for those who would know nothing but judgment, except you plead their case. They have no case of their own, but because of My love for you, I will hear your prayers and deliver even those whose hands are not innocent. Instead I will turn their deserved destruction into purifying fires, and they shall know of the One Whom they now despise.

Even as the principalities and powers know your fruit, so shall I use it to save an entire city by the prayers of even one righteous person. You have suffered great shame at their hands. But I will turn their curses into your blessing and all evil will be ashamed to stand in your presence.

"He will even deliver one who is not innocent; yes, he will be delivered by the purity of your hands." (Job 22:30 NKJV)

"And he saw that there was no man, and wondered that there was no intercessor: therefore his arm brought salvation unto him; and his righteousness, it sustained him." (Isa 59:16 KJV)

BIBLE STUDY OF ISAIAH 58 - GOD'S CHOSEN FAST

(Taken from the book 101+ Ways God Speaks And How To Hear Him, by Sandy Warner) swauthor@usa.net @ www.thequickenedword.com

Fasting is a strong sacrifice and bears much weight against the kingdom of darkness. Fasting is a form of denying oneself and following in the Lord's footsteps.

~ ISAIAH 58 - THE FORMAT OF GOD'S FAST ~
"Is this not the fast that I have chosen: To loose the bonds of wickedness, To undo the heavy burdens, To let the oppressed go free, And that you break every yoke?" (Isaiah 58:6 NKJV)

1. SHARE YOUR SUSTENANCE WITH THE NEEDY *(verse 7)*

Literal:
a. Divide your bread with the hungry
b. Bring the homeless poor into your house
c. When you see the naked, to cover him
d. Don't hide yourself from your own flesh
Spiritual:
a. Share God's Words with those in famine
b. Pray for the captive to come home
c. Forgive and cover your brother's sin
d. Pray for your family

2. TAKE AWAY OPPRESSIVE HEAVINESS *(Verse 9b)*

Literal:
a. Remove the yoke from your midst
b. Remove the pointing of the finger
c. Remove speaking wickedness

Spiritual:
a. Don't oppress others - not only in deed, but in thought and
      expectations
b. Do not criticize or judge your brother's walk
c. Pray and think kind words

3. SPEND YOUR OWN ENERGY FOR THE NEEDY *(verse 10 NASB)*

Literal:
a. Give yourself to the hungry
b. Satisfy the desire of the afflicted

Spiritual:
a. Lay aside your own goals for those hungry for God
b. Give hope to those in torment

~ THE PROMISES OF GOD'S FAST ~
1. LOOSE THE DARKNESS *(verse 8 and 10B)*

Physical, spiritual or emotional deliverance from darkness:
a. Your light will break out like the dawn
b. Your light will rise in the darkness
c. Your gloom will become like midday

2. QUICK HEALING *(verse 8 NASB)*

Healing for body, mind, soul, emotions, spirit:
a. Your recovery will speedily spring forth

3. YOUR RELATIONSHIP WITH HIM WILL GUIDE YOU
(verse 8B, 11, 9)

He will answer your plea for understanding:
a. Your righteousness will go before you
b. The glory of the Lord will be your rear guard
c. You will call, and the Lord will answer
d. You will cry, and He will say, Here am I

4. QUENCH THIRST AND STRENGTH *(verse 11)*

In trying times, He will give physical and spiritual strength and refreshment:
a. He will satisfy your desire in scorched places
b. And give strength to your bones
c. You will be like a watered garden
d. Like a spring of water whose waters do not fail

5. RESTORATION OF THE FALLEN *(verse 12 NASB)*

You will repair other's brokenness:
a. Those from among you will rebuild the ruins
b. You will rise up the age-old foundations
c. You will be called the repairer of the breach
d. The restorer of the streets in which to dwell

~ THE RESULT AND PURPOSE OF THE FAST ~

1. DELIVERANCE *(verse 6 NASB)*

Break satan's chains that immobilize, restrict, and restrain us from freedom:
a. Loosen the bonds of wickedness
b. Undo the bands of the yoke
c. Let the oppressed go free
d. Break every yoke

"If My people who are called by My name will humble themselves, and pray and seek My face, and turn from their

wicked ways, then I will hear from heaven, and will forgive their sin and heal their land. (2 Chronicles 7:14 NKJ)

SUMMARY ISAIAH 58 FAST:
Humility before the Lord and before one another When the heart is right before the Lord, one will not oppress others, or seek self satisfaction, as recorded in Isaiah 58:3. When the true humility before the Lord comes from the heart, it will show on the outside. For instance how we live and treat others.

In summary, the promises of the fast the Lord chooses in Isaiah 58 are to disperse darkness, quicken healing, provide guidance, quench thirst, restore strength and restore that which has fallen.

How to Intercede

HOW TO BATTLE SAFELY

Sometimes we can get ourselves in hot water when we do not understand how to pray for our city, and safely take authority over it. We are in a war, and we can expect some suffering as a part of the package. (2 Tim 2:3) However there are things that open the door to backlash and we can learn to war without excessive suffering.

~ HOW TO FIGHT A SAFER BATTLE ~
1. PRAY FOR PEACE
Just like praying for the peace of Jerusalem (Ps 122:6), we can pray for the peace of our city. A guest speaker recently said that he had gone to Ireland several years ago when it was in great conflict. When he returned, he found a totally different city. The troops were gone, people felt safe in the streets and the heavy spiritual oppression was gone. He asked the spiritual leaders about this and they shared their secret. They had sent little prayer teams to walk the streets

praying for peace... for 8 years. That's all they prayed and it worked!

2. PRAY FOR GOD'S WILL ON EARTH
If we only knew how vital prayer was, we would never stop praying. (I Thess 5:17, Phil 4:6) It is the pipeline that brings heaven to earth. Prayer is a safe and powerful weapon to make a difference for our cities without causing strong enemy retaliation. We are to pray that God's kingdom comes to earth and His will be done in our city. In these last days it is God's will that His glory shine upon the earth, all enemies come under His/our feet, and that all men might be saved. (Matt 6:10, Eze 43:2, Isa 60, Hag 2:7, I Cor 15:25, Rom 16:20, John 3:17)

3. PRAY FOR OUR LEADERS
We are all called to pray and make requests for our leaders. (I Tim 2:2,3) There is a reason for this. All of heaven, both angels and demons operate under a hierarchy of authority working down from the greatest to the least. The same government principle operates on earth and the enemy understands this, therefore he targets leaders because it gives him the greatest area of influence. Leaders on earth have the spiritual authority (both good and evil) to open spiritual doors to bless or curse those whom they govern. We need to raise up the standard of prayer for our leaders so their authority will be used to bless and protect. We can forgive their sins, then pray for their repentance and God's mercy, revelation, wisdom, integrity, Godly counsel, protection, salvation, etc. Praying for our leaders is a very powerful weapon against darkness.

4. PRAY IN TONGUES
When we pray in tongues, we are praying the mysteries of God because our minds do not understand what we are praying. (1 Cor 14:14-15) "Likewise the Spirit also helps in our weaknesses. For we do not know what we should pray for as we ought, but the Spirit Himself makes intercession for

us with groanings which cannot be uttered. Now He who searches the hearts knows what the mind of the Spirit is, because He makes intercession for the saints according to the will of God." (Rom 8:26-28 NKJV) We can pray in tongues over our city and know in confidence we are praying the mystery and will of God. I have had some of my best warfare breakthroughs, during or right after I have earnestly prayed in tongues.

5. SACRIFICE

In these last days many will become volunteer intercessors where they are willing to sacrifice to stand in the gap for their city. If we understood how powerful just one intercessor is, we would all volunteer, no matter what the cost. (Est 4:16) Each act of intercession is a mighty tool and makes a difference in conquering enemy territory. There are many forms of sacrifice, and too numerous to mention. Sacrifice is basically giving up something we deem valuable, and offering it to the Lord to use for His purposes.

6. WORSHIP

Psalms 149 says the high praises of God in our mouth and a two edged sword in our hand brings judgment upon the enemy and binds their rulers with chains. (These swords are the Word of God. Eph 6:17, Heb 4:12, Rev 1:16, 19:15) In this Psalms, he tells us to praise Him in dance, song, tambourines and stringed instruments. Worship is a powerful tool in warfare. I have been in meetings where the worship is so powerful that people are delivered without any hands-on ministry. Demons can't stand to hear the high praises of our Lord Jesus Christ! I have also seen people delivered when I waved my tambourine over them during worship.

HOW TO OCCUPY

A REVELATORY TEACHING ON THE DIFFERENCE BETWEEN STRETCHING AND ENLARGING

10/13/06: I received the following revelation during a prayer meeting where a group of people were powerfully praying in tongues against the demonic in our area, backing one who was taking authority in English.

HEARD: *Jabez.*

PIX: *I saw a rubberband.*

IMPRESSION: I had the impression of a rubber band being stretched out, then when let go, it bounces right back into place.

QUICKENED MEMORY: The Lord brought back the memory of the scripture:

Isa 54:2-3 NKJV
"Enlarge the place of your tent, and let them stretch out the curtains of your dwellings; Do not spare; Lengthen your cords, and strengthen your stakes. For you shall expand to the right and to the left, and your descendants will inherit the nations, and make the desolate cities inhabited.

I realized that stretching has a tension and a pressure added, and it can reach out, and then come back in. It is just like the skirts of a tent. The tent has a certain boundary, which has a limit to which it can stretch its skirts.

HEARD: *Maintain what you have obtained.*

MEMORY: When you go on a fast, you put all of your resources and time towards that goal, but you can't keep it up. Same with stretching to go on a diet, if you return to your old ways, it all bounces back. Same with striving for straight A's on a report card. If it is not a part of your natural abilities, as soon as you let up a tad, your grades fall back to your natural abilities.

It was quickened to me to look up the Jabez scripture:

1 Chron 4:10 KJV
And Jabez called on the God of Israel, saying, Oh that thou wouldest bless me indeed, and enlarge my coast, and that thine hand might be with me, and that thou wouldest keep me from evil, that it may not grieve me! And God granted him that which he requested.

1 Chron 4:10 AMP
Jabez cried to the God of Israel, saying, Oh, that You would bless me and enlarge my border, and that Your hand might be with me, and You would keep me from evil so it might not hurt me! And God granted his request.

WORD STUDY

OT:7337 ENLARGE

OT:7337 rachab (raw-khab'); a primitive root; to broaden (intransitive or transitive, literal or figurative):

KJV - be an en- make) large (-ing), make room, make (open) wide.

OT:1366 COAST OR BOUNDARY

OT:1366 gebuwl (gheb-ool'); or (shortened) gebul (gheb-ool'); from OT:1379; properly, a cord (as twisted), i.e. (by implication) a boundary; by extens. the territory inclosed:

KJV - border, bound, coast, great, landmark, limit, quarter, space.

THE MOMENT OF REVELATION: When I read the words, "enlarge my coast" I suddenly realized that the coast lines are pre-determined boundaries and that when the boundaries are enlarged, they actually move and change instead of just stretch.

QUICKENED MEMORY:

Deut 32:8 NLT
When the Most High assigned lands to the nations, when he divided up the human race, he established the boundaries of the peoples according to the number of **angelic beings.

**1121 !Be ben {bane}

Meaning: 1) son, grandson, child, member of a group 1a) son, male child 1b) grandson 1c) children (pl. - male and female) 1d) youth, young men (pl.) 1e) young (of animals) 1f) sons (as characterisation, ie sons of injustice [for un-righteous men] or sons of God [for angels] 1g) people (of a nation) (pl.) 1h) of lifeless things, ie sparks, stars, arrows (fig.) 1i) a member of a guild, order, class

Origin: from 01129; TWOT - 254; n m

Usage: AV - son 2978, children 1568, old 135, first 51, man 20, young 18, young + 01241 17, child 10, stranger 10, people 5, misc 92; 4906

EXPERIENCE; As warriors we were all strongly praying in tongues and also taking authority against specific demonic spirits in our area. I felt a powerful sweeping motion against these spirits as they left.

MEMORY: Immediately I realized that just like driving demons out of a person, you must fill the hole, otherwise 7 more come back. I also had the impression that when we rise up in such powerful tongues in unity against these things, that it is also like stretching, that as soon as we let up, it leaves room for a dark oppression to return even worse than before. I suddenly understood that we must "occupy and grow into" the territory and maintain it, not just reach out and stretch into it.

[I remember Bob Jones saying that he no longer prays for revival, because once it dies out, the darkness that comes back to fill the void is much worse than before. So he prays for habitation instead.]

Matt 12:43-45 NLT
"When an evil spirit leaves a person, it goes into the desert, seeking rest but finding none. Then it says, 'I will return to the person I came from.' So it returns and finds its former home empty, swept, and clean. Then the spirit finds seven other spirits more evil than itself, and they all enter the person and live there. And so that person is worse off than before. That will be the experience of this evil generation."

[Lord how do we occupy this and how do we maintain this to keep this from happening?]

QUICKENED PRAYER: The Lord reminded me that in order to occupy we are working in synergy with the angels. So I prayed that the Lord would send an angel to mark out a new boundary line to hold back the demonic. This would keep them from sweeping back in once we let the pressure off from our unified tongues and warfare.

QUICKENED MEMORY: FILL THE GAP WITH THE RIGHTEOUS COUNTERPART: He then brought back the memory of what He told Rick Joyner, that whenever we chop down a tree, we must plant a righteous tree in its place, otherwise the old demonic one will grow back even stronger, as though merely pruned.

PRAY IN THE OPPOSITE SPIRIT: As I was asking the Lord how do we plant a righteous tree/ spirit to replace what we drive out of our area? And He reminded me of the principal of praying in the opposite spirit. If we are driving out unbelief, we loose faith to replace it. If we are driving out agitation and unrest, we pray for and loose peace to be planted in its stead.

PIX: *I saw a stake in the ground, as though a claim for territory.*

I realized that having an angel posted at the boundary and planting a tree of the opposite of what we drove out, IS like claiming our territory, putting that stake in the ground.

TAKE AUTHORITY THAT THEY RETURN NO MORE:

Mark 9:25-26 NKJV
He rebuked the unclean spirit, saying to it, "Deaf and dumb spirit, I command you, come out of him and enter him no more !"

PRAYER: [Lord how to we occupy and maintain this new place?] He brought into memory the following scriptures.

QUICKENED MEMORY:

Deut 11:24 NKJV
Every place on which the sole of your foot treads shall be yours:

Josh 1:3-7 NKJV
Every place that the sole of your foot will tread upon I have given you, as I said to Moses. From the wilderness and this Lebanon as far as the great river, the River Euphrates, all the land of the Hittites, and to the Great Sea toward the going down of the sun, shall be your territory. No man shall

be able to stand before you all the days of your life; as I was with Moses, so I will be with you. I will not leave you nor forsake you. Be strong and of good courage, for to this people you shall divide as an inheritance the land which I swore to their fathers to give them.

Ex 23:29-33 NKJV
I will not drive them out from before you in one year, lest the land become desolate and the beasts of the field become too numerous for you. Little by little I will drive them out from before you, until you have increased, and you inherit the land. And I will set your bounds from the Red Sea to the sea, Philistia, and from the desert to the River. For I will deliver the inhabitants of the land into your hand, and you shall drive them out before you. You shall make no covenant with them, nor with their gods. They shall not dwell in your land, lest they make you sin against Me. For if you serve their gods, it will surely be a snare to you."

REVELATION: I understood that the way we occupy this new territory that is swept away from the demonic is literally to walk into it. The authority to MAINTAIN what we have OBTAINED by faith, is to walk in that authority. **It is very simple. If we do not walk in the opposite spirit of what we loosed, then we can not keep that ground. To the same level of integrity that we walk in our life, is the same level of integrity we maintain**.

John 5:14 NKJV
"See, you have been made well. Sin no more, lest a worse thing come upon you."

Lev 26:23-24 NKJV
'And if by these things you are not reformed by Me, but walk contrary to Me, then I also will walk contrary to you, and I will punish you yet seven times for your sins.

Matt 12:45 NKJV
Then he goes and takes with him seven other spirits more wicked than himself, and they enter and dwell there; and the

last state of that man is worse than the first. So shall it also be with this wicked generation."

CONFIRMATION: One of our intercessors when praying over our local university, called forth the seeds of the many prayer walks given on the school grounds. This was a good connection to the revelation of how to occupy.

SUMMARY: We want to expand our borders, not just stretch them. We do this by:

1. Warring and driving the demonic out.

2. Posting angels to keep the ground.

3. Praying in the opposite spirit by loosing the righteous counterpart to be planted in their stead.

4. Commanding the demonic not return.

5. Walking in the Spirit of what we have planted or loosed, fearing God lest we lose ground by our sin or even by allowing our walk to agree with what we drove out.

Lord thank You for this revelation, please train us in this so we can cooperate with You and Your heavenly hosts. in Jesus Name.

TO PARTNER WITH HIM IN PRAYER

From the passion of Your bosom,
I feel the heartbeats of Your love.
How you continue to incubate,
I know not how or of.

But Your Words just keep on flowing
With understanding and knowing.
They pour out upon the earth -
Your giant womb yet to give birth.

101

The times and seasons are in Your great hands.
It's not in the agenda or hands of man.
In the fullness of time, ripe, they burst forth.
Carried forth by angels on wings that soar.

Each Word is nurtured and coddled with care,
With men and angels united so rare.
Spanning Your bridge as from heaven to earth,
Each Word is a jewel, destined with worth.

Let Your will be done on earth as in heaven,
Your grace is sufficient to take out leaven.
To guard and to keep what is absolute Thine
Kept pure and holy even as it's refined.

Please impart us this day our daily bread
Let Your manna fall that we may be fed.
We sup at Your table drinking Your cup,
We lean into You to hear what is up.

Grant us ears to hear and grant eyes to see
That we may partner, uniting with Thee.
As we labor to enter with trust and belief
Grant understanding, providing relief.

We desire to please You with our effort,
God forbid that what we carry might abort.
We are weak at most and ignorant at best
To know how to nurture and guard our own nest.

We wait upon You to train us to defend.
Our backs are together looking out and in.
To protect from marauder's attempt to fear.
And to see the young incubating so near.

Yes birds of a feather do flock together,
Waiting for loved ones whose feet are still tethered.
Given tasks to perform while we are waiting,
While the demonic floods are still abating.

The earth is drying from our time in Your ark,
With anticipation we're waiting to embark.
Not in, but out, Your door of eminent hope,
Promised to the prophets, as seen through their scope.

We'll come out Your door with families intact
Prepared to gather anything we lack.
The slates wiped clean with pure new beginnings,
From disciplined lives, repentant from sinning.

Jesus' blood and grace is more than enough
To keep us from stumbling from rocks too rough.
We hold the hands of the weak and feeble,
Bringing them along making sure they're able.

Bravely taking the journey to our new land,
United, moving on, and making our stand.
What a joy to witness our promised new place
Prosperous and healthy, poured from Your grace.

So as we wait by our nest in Your vast love,
We will rest in Your hope and plan from above.
That our loved ones are incubating, safe and sound
As we declare Your great Words, that they may abound.

Hos 2:14-16 NLT
"But then I will win her back once again. I will lead her out into
the desert and speak tenderly to her there. I will return her
vineyards to her and transform the Valley of Trouble into gateway
of hope. She will give herself to me there, as she did long ago when
she was young, when I freed her from her captivity in Egypt. "In
that coming day," says the LORD, "you will call me 'my husband'
instead of 'my master.'

HOW TO WATCH AND PRAY

REVELATION 2/03/08: Today I realized that when Jesus said to watch and pray it was in chronological order. To hear and see what the Father is doing first, and then pray it.

WORD O' GRAM WATCH AND THEN PRAY 2/03/08

Waiting on the Lord

Altogether focused while

Thoughtfully listening for His voice.

Considering His Words

Heeding to what I see and hear.

AND THEN

Pouring out my

Response to what I have seen and heard.

Aligning heaven's Words onto earth.

Yielding my words to His.

Matt 26:40-41 NKJV
Then He came to the disciples and found them sleeping, and said to Peter, "What! Could you not watch with Me one hour? Watch and pray , lest you enter into temptation. The spirit indeed is willing, but the flesh is weak."

RHEMA 1/05/08 IT TAKES TWO: WATCH AND PRAY

HEARD: *Your new home. Here's what I have for you. Affordable. Understand how this works. It takes two.*

Matt 18:18-20 NKJV

"Assuredly, I say to you, whatever you bind on earth will be bound in heaven, and whatever you loose on earth will be loosed in heaven. "Again I say to you that if two of you agree on earth concerning anything that they ask, it will be done for them by My Father in heaven. 20 For where two or three are gathered together in My name, I am there in the midst of them."

HEARD: *Go quickly and tell her the good news. Pray. The great plan, we will watch together. An alliance. Window. See and understand. Together.*

HEARD: *The power of the spoken word.*

PIX: *I saw a scrabble game where the letters had been carefully laid down and scores were tallied.*

=======

COME LET US PRAY 1/14/08

DREAM: *I was in a group of about 20 people and said, "Who among you have led prayer meetings? I am sure you have each kicked yourself afterwards about what you could have said, would have said, should have said...and didnt say. All that God wants from us is for us to pour out our hearts to Him. Each one of us has a gift of unique expression that God has planted within us. Come now, let's pray!"*

1 Cor 12:4-7 NLT
Now there are different kinds of spiritual gifts, but it is the same Holy Spirit who is the source of them all. 5 There are different kinds of service in the church, but it is the same Lord we are serving. 6 There are different ways God works in our lives, but it is the same God who does the work through all of us. 7 A spiritual gift is given to each of us as a means of helping the entire church.

=======

ACCOUNTABLE TO PRAY 11/18/06

INTERCESSOR'S VISION: One of our intercessors saw a vision where a man who used to pray a lot was in front row of a room of about 50. It was his responsibility to pray for those people. He was no longer praying. Then the intercessor saw that each one of those 50 people also had other rooms of 50 people they prayed for. When the first one stopped praying, it affected all the others. "When a leader stops praying over his flock of 50, then it not only affects those 50, but also the 50 that each one of those are also called to keep. Am I my brother's keeper? YES."

CONFIRMATION: During the same prayer meeting, another intercessor told me that she heard the words, "PRAY, PRAY, PRAY."

SIMPLE PRAYER, RESTING FAITH

SIMPLE, HUMBLE PRAYER

The Lord has mentioned prayer to me several times this year. There are many kinds of prayers and intercessors. There are loud prayers, soft prayers, silent prayers, written prayers, song prayers, instrument prayers, poetry prayers, tongues prayers, groaning and yearning prayers, living prayers and even wishful thinking prayers. I am also sure there are more kinds of prayers. I believe that the Lord is so desperate for our prayers, that He turns most anything into a prayer, including our heart's desires, when our hearts are turned toward Him.

I attend lots of prayer meetings and those times are always loud, powerful and dynamic when in the room with 30 other intercessors all praying in tongues and in agreement as they rotate in taking the lead in English. The Lord's Presence is strong and powerful. When I am by myself, most of the time I do not pray powerfully loud English prayers. I do pray out loud in tongues and English and receive some powerful breakthroughs, especially when I pray in the car or

106

exercising with the music!! But when I am at home during the day, I pray mostly quiet prayers or silent communion prayers. I had been thinking a lot about that and wondering if it was OK to pray that way, since it is my habit. In answer to my ponderings about this, here is some of the rhema I received this month:

RHEMA 10/01/06 SEATED PRAYER
[I had just prayed a 2 sentence prayer, it was exactly to the point and nothing else.]

HEARD: *You pray so well dear Sweetheart, that's all I need. My safe one. Come let us pray, find out how. Seat yourself. You understand. Resting faith.*

Heb 4:1-12 NLT
God's promise of entering his place of rest still stands, so we ought to tremble with fear that some of you might fail to get there. For this Good News — that God has prepared a place of rest — has been announced to us just as it was to them. But it did them no good because they didn't believe what God told them. For only we who believe can enter his place of rest.

As for those who didn't believe, God said, "In my anger I made a vow: 'They will never enter my place of rest,' "even though his place of rest has been ready since he made the world. We know it is ready because the Scriptures mention the seventh day, saying, "On the seventh day God rested from all his work." But in the other passage God said, "They will never enter my place of rest." So God's rest is there for people to enter. But those who formerly heard the Good News failed to enter because they disobeyed God. So God set another time for entering his place of rest, and that time is today.

God announced this through David a long time later in the words already quoted: "Today you must listen to his voice. Don't harden your hearts against him."

This new place of rest was not the land of Canaan, where Joshua led them. If it had been, God would not have spoken later about another day of rest. So there is a special rest still waiting for the people of God. For all who enter into God's rest will find rest from their labors, just as God rested after creating the world. Let us do our best to enter that place of rest. For anyone who disobeys God, as the people of Israel did, will fall. For the word of God is full of living power. It is sharper than the sharpest knife, cutting deep into our innermost thoughts and desires.

RHEMA 11/01/06 RESTING PRAYER

HEARD: *Ought to pray, as often as you like.*

PIX: *I saw a beautiful woman bathing in an old fashioned bathtub full of glistening bubbles. Her head was tilted back looking up to heaven. She was so lovely and peaceful and relaxed.*

HEARD: *That's how I want you to pray. Swing vote. You voted, My love, it was your decision. Joy. Laughing, eternity.*

COMMENT: I love to pray in the bathtub, when relaxing. When He was speaking to me about the swing vote, He was talking to me about being a doorkeeper. This is where we make our decisions about right and wrong on the earth, and we declare open doors to what we see as right. And this is where we speak close doors to what we see that does not line up with His will on earth. Being a doorkeeper and casting our vote is like a prayer, only with more authority. A doorkeeper prayer can be a supplication where we ask the Lord to open or close a door. However, the position of actually being a doorkeeper, where we have a place of authority in our family, or job, or elsewhere, is where we can declare into the spirituals that the doors be open or shut.

When He spoke to me about being this doorkeeper, He was saying that I don't need to be loud or stressful in casting my vote. Have you ever cast your ballot in the bathtub? Smile.

Isa 22:22-23 NKJV
The key of the house of David I will lay on his shoulder; So he shall open, and no one shall shut; And he shall shut, and no one shall open. I will fasten him as a peg in a secure place, And he will become a glorious throne to his father's house.

CONFIRMATION: I just went to the forum to get this link that is a teaching about being a Doorkeeper. The random graphic that popped onto the top of the screen was the one about the doorkeeper.

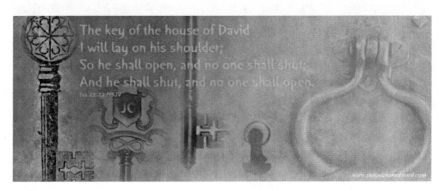

RHEMA 11/06/06 HUMBLE PRAYER

HEARD: *The gift of prayer. Freedom. To hold you accountable and release the angels. To do what you are to do. There is mercy at the core.*

HEARD: *Having said it all, just rest.*

HEARD: *Low bridge.*

(Humility, bowing low.)

COMMENT: The Lord is saying that every time we pray, we are giving a gift. Prayer is like a bridge that gives His kingdom and people a chance to safely cross over the obstacles. Yes, we are accountable to pray and bring His kingdom to earth and when we pray it releases the angels to go forth and bring freedom. He is also saying that our having known the need for prayer, that no matter how much we pray and fall short in such, He grants us mercy. And once we have prayed and gained the witness that He has heard and will answer, we REST. As the scripture says, He honors humble, repentant prayer.

2 Chron 7:13-14 NKJV
...if My people who are called by My name will humble themselves, and pray and seek My face, and turn from their wicked ways, then I will hear from heaven, and will forgive their sin and heal their land...

~ SIMPLE INTERCESSION ~

I am a simple intercessor who, when the Lord tells me things, I write them down and hold onto them like Mary in my heart, waiting to see it manifested on earth. Most of the time, I also walk these things out in misc. parables that connect with His Words, and I also have to stand against all the obstacles that oppose the Words I have heard. This kind of intercession is more of a walking and abiding place then it is verbalizing long prayers. These are intercessions I do not share with the public, and if I am led to, I share them through simple Words to Ponder, as the Holy Spirit leads.

Matt 6:5-7 NKJV
But you, when you pray, go into your room, and when you have shut your door, pray to your Father who is in the secret place; and your Father who sees in secret will reward you openly. And when you pray, do not use vain repetitions as the heathen do. For they think that they will be heard for their many words.

CONFIRMATION: I had sent the above paragraph about simple intercession to a friend, and he wrote back saying that he saw a vision of the word "Simple" the same day.

Hi Sandy,
Thank you for sharing your precious word and PIX with me. In a vision, I clearly saw the word, "SIMPLE" clearly in a paper yesterday. The word "SIMPLE" was quickened to me when reading and I felt that it was connected to "the Kingdom of God". His Kingdom consists of those who are simple and humble like kids. Those who are the humblest are the highest in His Kingdom.

With His love and Kindness
{Name}

HEARD: *Precious child. Remember. All it takes is just one prayer. You are carrying so much of a load. Building.*

If you pray, you will be garrisoned and guarded by God's peace through Jesus Christ. If you pray, you will be set "at one" with Him.

Phil 4:6-7 AMP
Do not fret or have any anxiety about anything, but in every circumstance and in everything, by prayer and petition (definite requests), with thanksgiving, continue to make your wants known to God. 7 And God's peace [shall be yours, that tranquil state of a soul assured of its salvation through Christ, and so fearing nothing from God and being content with its earthly lot of whatever sort that is, that peace] which transcends all understanding shall garrison and mount guard over your hearts and minds in Christ Jesus.

RHEMA 11/28/06 CONTEND FOR THE FAITH, NO NEED TO STRIVE FOR IT

111

HEARD: *The gift of prayer. You can do this.*

QUICKENED FROM BOBBY CONNER: "He told me He was going to give me my report card and it was going to be sealed. He didnt tell me it was going to be sealed so that no one could see it, but it was going to be sealed in laminate so that no one could change it."

Bobby then said that he passed all the subjects except that he failed recess. He said it was because he never learned the difference between striving and contending. Contending is the work of the Spirit, striving is the work of the flesh. It is God's peace that crushes satan.

http://www.bobbyconner.org

Jude 3 NKJV
...exhorting you to contend earnestly for the faith.

CONTEND
epagonizomai

NT:1864 epagonizomai (ep-ag-o-nid'-zom-ahee); from NT:1909 and NT:75; to struggle for:
KJV - earnestly contend foreign

Matt 12:18-19 KJV
I will put my spirit upon him, and he shall shew judgment to the Gentiles. He shall not strive , nor cry; neither shall any man hear his voice in the streets.

Isa 45:9 KJV
Woe unto him that striveth with his Maker! Let the potsherd strive with the potsherds of the earth. Shall the clay say to him that fashioneth it, What makest thou? or thy work, He hath no hands?

PRAYING OUT LOUD OR SILENT?

PIX 5/30/06: *I saw a knife being drawn out of its long sword sheaf. I then saw a knight go down on one knee.*

HEARD: *How to pray.*

QUESTION: Lord do I need to pray out loud?

IMMEDIATE IMPRESSION: The Holy Spirit downloaded me with the memory of these 2 scriptures:

John 11:41-43 NKJV
And Jesus lifted up His eyes and said, "Father, I thank You that You have heard Me. And I know that You always hear Me , but because of the people who are standing by I said this, that they may believe that You sent Me."

John 12:27-31 NKJV
"Now My soul is troubled, and what shall I say? 'Father, save Me from this hour'? But for this purpose I came to this hour. Father, glorify Your name." Then a voice came from heaven, saying, "I have both glorified it and will glorify it again."
Therefore the people who stood by and heard it said that it had thundered. Others said, "An angel has spoken to Him." Jesus answered and said, "This voice did not come because of Me, but for your sake .

WORD TO PONDER: COMMUNION AND DECLARATION 5/30/06

Throughout the ages, I have heard mankind's questions about which is more effective, silent prayers or voiced prayers? Remember when on earth, I communed with My Father and He heard Me always, whether out loud or within My thoughts. And I heard My Father, whether out loud or in My thoughts. Prayer is simply communion and intimacy and can be enjoyed either way.

When I spoke to the fig tree, I spoke to it. When I declared to Lazarus in the grave, I spoke with a loud voice. When I agonized in the garden, My disciples heard My sufferings. When on the cross, I cried out to My Father in anguish of spirit, body and soul.

How may I answer you, dear one? I want you to express yourself in the best way you can express yourself. I hear you and listen.

1 Chron 28:9 NKJV
As for you, my son Solomon, know the God of your father, and serve Him with a loyal heart and with a willing mind; for the LORD searches all hearts and understands all the intent of the thoughts . If you seek Him, He will be found by you;

John 11:41-43 NKJV
And Jesus lifted up His eyes and said, "Father, I thank You that You have heard Me. And I know that You always hear Me , but because of the people who are standing by I said this, that they may believe that You sent Me."

John 12:27-31 NKJV
"Now My soul is troubled, and what shall I say? 'Father, save Me from this hour'? But for this purpose I came to this hour. Father, glorify Your name." Then a voice came from heaven, saying, "I have both glorified it and will glorify it again."

Therefore the people who stood by and heard it said that it had thundered. Others said, "An angel has spoken to Him." Jesus answered and said, "This voice did not come because of Me, but for your sake.

PRAYER THROUGH POETRY

HEARD 4/11/07: *Wife. She was sent with seeds in her belly.*

PIX: *I saw a women making her way through invisible vines. They were hard to forge through, but she was making* *progress. Each time she made one step, then wait on God. In the horizon was the ocean.*

"Who defined the boundaries of the sea as it burst from the womb, and as I clothed it with clouds and thick darkness? For I locked it behind barred gates, limiting its shores. I said, `Thus far and no farther will you come. Here your proud waves must stop!' (Job 38:8-11 NLT)

HEARD: *She's finding out about the intercession. They were in the form of poetry. I can feel it.*

TEACH ME TO PRAY

Oh Lord, when I give You little time,
Tell me, how can I expect Your prime?
Yet waiting to listen from afar,
Faithful as always, yes, there You are.

My life blurs before me in a hurry.
How can I pray when I am unworthy?
That is just the point that You try to say.
It's not what I deserve, it's what I pray.

You long to give me the desires of my heart.
Yet wounded from delay I'm unable to start.
I've learned to cope with a limp in my walk.
I've learned to withhold my heart from deep talk.

Teach me to pray and to become really real.
You said to believe and I'd have what I will.
So please still remind me always to ask.
As I learn to lean and take off my mask.

You said to confess to one another,
Our weakness, our need, to our brother.
The prayers of the righteous do avail much.
Teach me to receive their gracious touch.

Draw to the surface what needs to discuss.
Lance all the wounds and draw out the puss.
It hurts, this I know, to be real and raw
But that is grace, the other side of law.

Oh to be free to tell it like it is!
This is not a test, this is not a quiz.
It's just simple sharing what I need most,
And then You dispatch Your glorious host.

Either from my requests or from my brother.
You hear it all as we tell one another.
Thank You, dear Lord, as You teach me to pray.
As I lean and unveil my heart this day.

James 5:16 TLB
Admit your faults to one another and pray for each other so that
you may be healed. The earnest prayer of a righteous man has
great power and wonderful results.

INTERCESSION IS IMPORTUNITY

TEACHING: WHAT IS IMPORTUNITY?

The following scripture is importunity:

Luke 18:1-8 NLT
One day Jesus told his disciples a story to illustrate their
need for constant prayer and to show them that they must
never give up. 2 "There was a judge in a certain city," he
said, "who was a godless man with great contempt for
everyone. 3 A widow of that city came to him repeatedly,
appealing for justice against someone who had harmed her.
4 The judge ignored her for a while, but eventually she wore
him out. 'I fear neither God nor man,' he said to himself, 5'but
this woman is driving me crazy. I'm going to see that she
gets justice, because she is wearing me out with her
constant requests!' " 6 Then the Lord said, "Learn a lesson
from this evil judge. 7 Even he rendered a just decision in

the end, so don't you think God will surely give justice to his chosen people who plead with him day and night? Will he keep putting them off? 8 I tell you, he will grant justice to them quickly! But when I, the Son of Man, return, how many will I find who have faith?"

The past few years we were in a season of importunity, which was incessant knocking. This was a 2 way reciprocation where God was incessantly knocking upon our doors, calling, wooing, challenging, desperate and intense for us to wake up and become prepared for the days ahead. He has been so insistent that in His unfathomable love He bypassed our tolerances and boundaries in order to wake us up and get our attention. It was like shaking someone awake who has been in a long slumber.

This incessant knocking has not been only one way, for we too have been persistently knocking on His doors, trying and testing His tolerance by our same repeated prayers, the same desires, the same heart for Him to answer us with His YES and NOW. We have been like Jacob, wrestling with God to move Him past His boundaries and bring us the blessing. We were saying, You have something I want and you are not giving it to me! And God was saying, You have something I want and you are not giving it to Me either!

The word "intercessor" in the Old Testament means to make intercession through impinging importunity.

IMPINGE SYNONYMS: Impose, invade, to fall against; to strike; to dash against; to clash upon. Trespass, affect, bear upon, disturb, encroach, influence, infringe, intrude, invade, make inroads, obtrude, pry, touch, violate.

IMPORTUNITY SYNONYMS: coaxing, dunning, insistence, nagging, persistence, pestering, plaguing, plying, pressing, urgency, urging.

Isa 59:16 KJV

And he saw that there was no man, and wondered that there was no intercessor: {# 6293}

This Hebrew word is translated:
paga`
OT:6293 paga` (paw-gah'); a primitive root; **to impinge, by accident or violence, or (figuratively) by importunity:** KJV - come (betwixt), cause to entreat, fall (upon), make intercession, intercessor, intreat, lay, light [upon], meet (together), pray, reach, run.

Sometimes the Lord asks His intercessors to be an advocate and knock on doors on behalf of others. It can be a very humbling and non glorious job. The Lord will use the process to cleanse ones own soul through difficult circumstances and mistakes made. However, true to God's amazing way to using weak instruments, He will use it all as intercession through importunity. In the places where one dies to self will in place of His will, He would multiply all efforts of knocking on closed doors, to advance His kingdom on earth.

WORD TO PONDER: KNOCKING ON CLOSED DOORS 3/26/08
Yes precious ones, knocking on doors is a difficult job. You have walked through shame, and cast down your pride, embracing humility. You have walked through rejection and cast down ambition, embracing My passion. You have walked through innocent trust and disappointment in man's promises and cast down idolatry, embracing Me as your Source. You have walked through angry retorts and cast down fear of man, embracing forgiveness. You have walked through intimidation and cast down judgment, embracing holy boldness. You have walked through misunderstanding and cast down self defense, embracing your Just Judge. You have walked through an advocacy as a fool without dignity. You embraced considering yourself of no reputation. You have walked through the crushings of hopelessness, despair, loss of fellowship, abandonment, betrayal and much more. You have cast down your body, soul and spirit at My

feet to embrace death to self over and over again. In all that you have walked out, you chose to lovingly forgive and be the sacrifice for My call to knock until your job was done.

Even as you were willing to humble yourself to be used as a vessel of dishonor, I will grant you honor where honor is due. I know you did not seek honor, you sought My will above all else and were obedient to the faith I planted within you. Thank you beloved intercessors who have walked the road of importunity.

You have moved the depths of this Papa's heart, that inspite of everything, you still choose to love above all else. Through a multitude of knockings My door is opened and you have yet to fully realize that impact upon earth. Well done, beloved intercessors, enter in to the joy of your Lord.

2 Tim 2:20 KJV
But in a great house there are not only vessels of gold and of silver, but also of wood and of earth; and some to honour, and some to dishonour.

2 Sam 6:22 NKJV
And I will be even more undignified than this, and will be humble in my own sight.

1 Cor 13:7 NKJV
Love bears all things, love believes all things, love hopes all things, love endures all things.

PERSISTENCE IN PRAYER OPENS DOORS

One night as I was ready to go to sleep I kept asking the Lord if He had anything to say to me. I heard nothing. Then I asked again. Finally, I wasn't being very adult, and was really begging Him like a kid would do. One more time, I said, "PLLLLEEEEESE Lord?"

VISION: I saw the lines in a frownie face. The lines were being redrawn from the lips going down, to upwards in a smile. I laughed out loud and said Goodnight!

WORD TO PONDER: I WILL TURN YOUR FROWNS UP
Those frownie faces that do not become you shall one day be turned up into delighted smiles!

"The full soul loatheth an honeycomb; but to the hungry soul every bitter thing is sweet." (Prov 27:7 KJV)

=======

SANDY RHEMA

[Lord, it's me again. Please forgive me for nagging You so much, but I really want to hear from You.]

HEARD: *Words in My mouth.*

[Lord, You mean it's not nagging?]

HEARD: *Exactly the opposite. I am drawing you.*

============

NOTE: In hindsight, I think this next entry is quite humorous; it was before I was given a writing ministry.

EXPERIENCE: After hearing so little of late, I have grown very hungry and have been knocking continually for several days. Upon waking from another blank night, I asked the Lord what was going on. I thought of many possibilities, but nothing was planted in my heart. Then when I was getting ready for the day I heard the Lord say, "Encouragement." That was it.

I left for errands and then received the strangest Word. I was at the grocery store and heard the phrase, "Maybe she ought to know." I had the distinct feeling that either the Lord or some angels were speaking something about me. At that exact moment, a bakery lady with a giant clear plastic sack of fresh bread walked past me, carrying the bread over her shoulder. This was really quickened to me but I did not know why. Then later as I was driving home, I drove behind an "oversized load" truck on the freeway. I kept thinking about that oversize bread sack the lady was carrying and wondering what I was supposed to know. Well I haven't heard Him in days, I guess He is trying to send me encouragement.

============

GRANDMA ANNA RHEMA

HEARD: *I heard two knocks in the Spirit.*

HEARD: *Behold I stand at the door and knock. If any man hear My voice and open the door, I will come in to him and will sup with him and he with Me.*

HEARD: *Fear not little ones. It's the Father's good pleasure to give you the kingdom. Yes, it's a pearl of great price and you have the pearl encircled with your hands. The Kingdom of God suffers violence and you have taken it by force. Your importunity shall bring forth that which was otherwise impossible. You knocked, and knocked, and knocked. Finally the door opens. Be ye not troubled neither be ye afraid. Only believe.*

HEARD: *Importunity. Declare delivered. Make merry and be glad. Up and out. Through. Finished. The end. Amen. Blessed ones. Waiting for God. Thank you.*

============

BOB JONES QUOTE - ENTERING IN
http://www.bobjones.org

"...Don't talk to Him with the religious jargon. Just talk to Him with the truth, He already knows what's in your heart. If you had a bummer day, tell Him about it. If you are having problems, tell Him about it. You enter into the Presence of the Lord with faith, truth and inner honesty. These are 3 things that get you in there. First faith, then truth and be totally honest. And you are going to come into the Presence of the Lord. But I like to cultivate it. Through the years. It took me a while to get into it. But I believed and I kept seeking until I found. If you seek you will find. If you knock, the door will be opened to you. And sometimes my greatest knocking was silence. Shutting this off. (head) And you can, and listen. When it first starts, all these other phones in your mind are ringing all the time. And sometimes you don't hear until about 3 oclock at night when all the other phones have gone off. At 3 o clock at night this mind of yours is not doing the last day's work anymore and it hasn't started doing the next day's work. And your flesh has already rested from the last day. And it isn't hurting so bad you couldn't hear. Then is when you begin to get the light impressions. Then is when you need to listen. At first you need to write them down..."

=======

VISION 11/06/06: *I was going down the ramp to go underneath the stadium and someone said, "Describe the word, knock." And then an angel stood above me in the bleachers and looked at me and said, "Admirable." I looked up and said, "Thank you." It was a true compliment that I really received after having put so much effort in such.*

=======

WORD TO PONDER: SEEK ME
I can hear you knocking, dear one. I told you that you shall find Me if you seek Me. So why do you frown? Do you think I am lost? Smile, precious! I am not lost, but I do hide Myself. I draw your heart to earnestly seek Me with all your heart, so that you would know Me in all My ways. How I love to reveal My heart to those who are truly hungry for Me. Do not feel

guilty about your tendency to nag until I answer. I am drawing you and developing within you the habit of searching for Me, so that you will learn to abide in Me, and not stray from My side. I know that once you "catch" Me, you will never let go!

Luke 11:9-13 NLT
"And so I tell you, keep on asking, and you will be given what you ask for. Keep on looking, and you will find. Keep on knocking, and the door will be opened. For everyone who asks, receives. Everyone who seeks, finds. And the door is opened to everyone who knocks. "You fathers--if your children ask for a fish, do you give them a snake instead? Or if they ask for an egg, do you give them a scorpion? Of course not! If you sinful people know how to give good gifts to your children, how much more will your heavenly Father give the Holy Spirit to those who ask him."

PERSISTENCE, DON'T GIVE UP

VISION: *I saw my son's keys.*
HEARD: *Teach them to pray.*

Yesterday my son lost his keys in the house. We rarely lose things in our home, because it is so organized. (One of the reasons is because I can't stand looking for things!) So we turned the house upside down for those keys. All the while I kept saying, "Lord where are the keys?" We went to bed and still no keys. I continued to pray and asked the Lord if He would either tell me or show me a vision of where they were. As a result, the above is what I saw and heard! That was not exactly what I had in mind, but the Lord wanted an object lesson instead.

This morning as our son was getting ready for school, not only did he not find his keys, but he couldn't find his watch either. He said he would be lost at school without his watch and went to school in the mulli-grubs.

123

I woke up feeling like I was fighting a bug or the flu, but it was time to pick up the house. As I glanced at my table, there was an old outdated tape recorder and some tapes that did not belong on it. Because I felt so yucky, I didn't want to put it all away, but neither did I want to leave the mess on the table because it bothered me.

I took the recorder and put it on the kitchen counter. Then I looked at it on the counter and said, "That's stupid to clean the table and then clutter my counter!" So I dragged myself into the next room closer to our storage closet and dumped it on that table. I looked at that table and said, "You are almost there, just put it away!" I walked into the storage closet and dumped the old recorder into the box with the old earphone paraphernalia and recorder cords.

For some strange reason as I was doing it, I thought to myself, "Wouldn't it be terrible to dump this in the box, never looking inside the box, and all the time my son's keys are in there???" So even though I felt so weak and sickly, I lifted the box down from the high shelf and glanced at the contents. I saw no keys.

As I was starting to put the box back, I thought, "What if his keys are at the bottom of the box, and I stopped too short?" So I lifted the earphones and cords and there were the keys just waiting to be found! How they got there I did not know. I was quite amazed that the Lord has coaxed me one halting step at a time towards the bottom of that box.

This was most definitely a story of persistence. I could have stopped anywhere along the way, and every step was an overcoming one, because I felt so weak and sick. It was not an easy task, but in spite of myself, the Lord answered my prayers and drew me the whole way. I wondered how long it would have been if I had just dumped the recorder in the box without looking. It could have been months till we used that box again.

I told Wayne the story at lunch about finding the keys, and that now our son had also lost his watch. We prayed again. When he came home from school, he saw the keys hanging from the kitchen counter knob, where we usually paste little notes to him. He was grinning ear to ear and thanking the Lord. When he entered his bedroom, the Lord directed his eyes and they fell upon the crack between his storage chest and bed. You guessed it... his watch. As he came out a few minutes later, very happy, Wayne related a very exciting story!!!

Earlier he came in and asked me where his measuring tape was. I didn't know, and was feeling very wiped out and laying down so he searched by himself. Evidently he went into his shop a second time and said, "Lord the enemy is stealing from us and this needs to stop right now!" As soon as he said this, he looked down and saw the corner of his measuring tape sticking out of a place he had already searched.

WORD TO PONDER: PERSISTENCE RECOVERS ALL
Beloved ones, I know you are weary and frustrated with your losses. I AM drawing you to get your focus off your misery and begin to exercise through prayer, the rights I have given you. It is time to learn how to recover what has been stolen.

Ask Me for help to restore your losses. I seek and find that which is lost. Join Me! Be persistent in your faith until you get your rewards. Do not stop short of your goal, do not settle for less. Begin to put your foot down and command that what the enemy has stolen be returned.

Dear ones, I know you are weary, hurting and discouraged. Let go of the outdated tapes that repeat in your mind. Put the past behind you and don't give up. Be persistent. With one foot in front of the other, overcome one step at a time. Keep going, you are almost there. As you trust Me to answer your prayers, I will draw you along the right path in spite of yourself. If you do not give up, you shall recover all.

1 Sam 30:3-4,8 NLT
When David and his men saw the ruins and realized what had happened to their families, they wept until they could weep no more....Then David asked the LORD, "Should I chase them? Will I catch them?" And the LORD told him, "Yes, go after them. You will surely recover everything that was taken from you!"

The Burden of Prayer

BEAR ONE ANOTHER'S BURDENS

EXPERIENCE RHEMA 1/8/95: Sometimes the burden of intercession weighs heavy on the heart. The following is an incredible series of confirmations as relating to the burden of the Lord, as well as the heaviness of the anointing. Wayne asked me if I came in and prayed for him this morning before running business deliveries.

I told him as I was walking down the hall I prayed, "Lord help my husband today. I love him so much." It was a very tired, exhausted and weary prayer and I had been deeply carrying his burdens of his own illness. I was ailing yesterday and this morning I felt like I'd been through world war 9.

WAYNE'S VISION AND OPENING OF SENSES: Wayne then said I came in while he was sleeping on his stomach, and I knelt on the floor, laid horizontally across his back, and prayed for him. I relaxed my whole weight over him and he felt the 'UHMF' as he sunk under it. He thought I was praying, so he reached out and touched my arm, feeling my sweater and arm underneath. Because of the weight, and him knowing I had been sick yesterday with a migraine, he wasn't sure if he was holding my weariness up or I was praying for him!!

126

COMMENT: The parable was that Wayne in his opening of senses experience, could not discern who was carrying who, as he felt my weight, and my weight was the weight of carrying his burdens! Funny!

UPDATE COMMENT: It is also a parable of resurrection of the sleeping ones in the scripture:

2 Kings 4:33-35 NLT
He went in alone and shut the door behind him and prayed to the LORD. 34 Then he lay down on the child's body, placing his mouth on the child's mouth, his eyes on the child's eyes, and his hands on the child's hands. And the child's body began to grow warm again! 35 Elisha got up and walked back and forth in the room a few times. Then he stretched himself out again on the child. This time the boy sneezed seven times and opened his eyes!

CONFIRMATION THE SAME DAY: After yesterday's sermon, Anna had a very heavy burden in which she was interceding for the church. As one of the elders caught her eye and tried to approach her, he spun around against the wall of the church. It happened a second time the same way. When they finally talked, he thought she needed prayer and she said she'd had a burden of intercession. He said he must have felt the weight of the burden she was carrying.

As Anna was relating this story to me over the phone, I had been working on formatting my rhema into italics. I got caught up in what she was saying, so I stopped, not realizing the sentence I'd stopped at. After she finished sharing it, my brain registered where my eyes were looking on the screen. The following bolded insert is what I had literally been staring at on the screen as she told me the story:

INSERT BURDENS: RHEMA 1/3/96: I had super heaviness in my spirit today. I prayed for Wayne knowing he was struggling. As I went to the PO I again prayed and I

HEARD: *Bear my brother's weight. Bear one another's burdens.*

Then tonight at dinner I told Wayne I felt much better and mentioned my grieving spirit. He said I was "bearing his burdens." I didn't tell him I'd heard the Lord say that too. Today as I was praying over the rhema "set him free for the period of transition" kept coming to mind. I was praying and warring over that Word so now that the burden is lifted I am hoping that God's sons have been set free for the upcoming transitions taking place.

Gal 6:3 NKJV
Bear one another's burdens , and so fulfill the law of Christ.

Num 11:10-15 NKJV
So Moses said to the LORD, "Why have You afflicted Your servant? And why have I not found favor in Your sight, that You have laid the burden of all these people on me? 12 Did I conceive all these people? Did I beget them, that You should say to me,'Carry them in your bosom, as a guardian carries a nursing child,' to the land which You swore to their fathers? 13 Where am I to get meat to give to all these people? For they weep all over me, saying, 'Give us meat, that we may eat.' 14 I am not able to bear all these people alone, because the burden is too heavy for me. 15 If You treat me like this, please kill me here and now — if I have found favor in Your sight — and do not let me see my wretchedness!"

Isa 58:6 NKJV
"Is this not the fast that I have chosen: To loose the bonds of wickedness, To undo the heavy burdens, To let the oppressed go free, And that you break every yoke?

Rom 15:1-2 NKJV
We then who are strong ought to bear with the scruples of the weak, and not to please ourselves. 2 Let each of us please his neighbor for his good, leading to edification.

1 John 5:3 NKJV

For this is the love of God, that we keep His commandments. And His commandments are not burdensome .

GROANING OVER THE ORPHANS

HEARD 12/29/06: *Yes I AM. It's ME. Capital M. You are adopted sweet one. You belong to Me, Your Papa. Comfort.*

HEARD 4/26/07: *Pure and undefiled religion is to visit the orphans and the widows. Thank you.*

James 1:27 NKJV
Pure and undefiled religion before God and the Father is this: to visit orphans and widows in their trouble, and to keep oneself unspotted from the world.

HEARD: *So many have no home Sweetheart. They simply move from here to there.*

Hungry.

Outside.

Moving

Endlessly.

Life's

Empty

Search for

Shelter.

CONFIRMATION: I was groaning today under prayer.

PRAYER: Abba, how grieved You are over the disjointed heart of Your family! How deeply You feel the pain over the wounds from loved ones and foes. How deeply You feel the suffering from compounded fractures left to heal in isolation and broken ditches in the road of life. Stranded and helpless, and lost without hope... those are the orphans that You groan over. And You are teaching us their pain, by suffering our own. How blessed we are Lord, and how little our pain is when we consider a life without You, without family and without a safe place to settle in Your safe arms of love!

Bring Your children home Lord, bring them in! Reach their hungry souls with Your bread. Go to the highways and byways of life and move endlessly until they are found and brought into Your house. Grant that these, Your orphans would no longer wander in empty searches for the shelter of Your love.

Luke 14:16-24 NKJV
Then He said to him, "A certain man gave a great supper and invited many, and sent his servant at supper time to say to those who were invited, 'Come, for all things are now ready.' But they all with one accord began to make excuses. The first said to him, 'I have bought a piece of ground, and I must go and see it. I ask you to have me excused.' And another said, 'I have bought five yoke of oxen, and I am going to test them. I ask you to have me excused.' Still another said, 'I have married a wife, and therefore I cannot come.' So that servant came and reported these things to his master. Then the master of the house, being angry, said to his servant, 'Go out quickly into the streets and lanes of the city, and bring in here the poor and the maimed and the lame and the blind.' And the servant said, 'Master, it is done as you commanded, and still there is room.' Then the master said to the servant, 'Go out into the highways and hedges, and compel them to come in, that my house may be filled. For I say to you that none of those men who were invited shall taste my supper.'"

You number my wanderings;
Put my tears into Your bottle; Are they not in Your book?
Ps 56:8 NKJV

www.thequickenedword.com

TEARS ARE PRECIOUS WORDS 12/30/07

When my heart is tender and I reflect upon precious times, sometimes my eyes water and my cheeks become wet and I haven't even noticed. They continue to fall as a natural reflection of unspoken words from deep within. They are words too deep to say, words only that my heart speaks as gentle rain upon my cheeks.

Other times when my heart is squeezed, its pain comes and goes as it ebbs and flows. As my bleeding heart pumps, it presses water from my eyes like the nectar of a crushed rose.

Sometimes I hear the joyous good news from a loved one and tears come once again. They are happy tears that burst forth like dancing fountains amidst the warmth of a summer day.

In every tear there is a word too precious to say. In every tear there is a heart that responds God's way. Upon every wet cheek there is a story. I am so glad that God collects our tears and they are precious to Him.

It is His prayer that the language of tears become precious to us too, and that we learn to embrace those who speak with wet cheeks.

Ps 56:8 NKJV
You number my wanderings; Put my tears into Your bottle; Are they not in Your book?

Ps 139:16-17 NKJV
Your eyes saw my substance, being yet unformed. And in Your book they all were written, the days fashioned for me, when as yet there were none of them. How precious also are Your thoughts to me, O God! How great is the sum of them!

TEARS OPENING THE HEAVENS

HEARD 11/13/06: *Release and set free. My beloved, do not be afraid. My fire bride.*

VISION: *I saw a Man approach me and He had something very strong in His eyes as He looked at me. He handed me something and I said thank you. It was the memory of His look, that was like a deep knowing me with great intensity and His approach was with controlled, but with passionate aggression.*

When out of the vision I did not remember His face, but I remember the feeling of His intense and passionate look upon me and I knew He knew Me inside and out. He wanted all of me.

HEARD: *You fit. Like a glove. I am teaching her and making her more vulnerable. Set her free with purity. Thank you for your tears. My friend. There's an open door above your head.*

PARABLE: At church I sat right next to the leak in the roof. When it rained hard, I saw drips, like tear drops fall onto the floor beside me.

HEARD: *Release the anointing to overflowing.*

PIX: *I saw a man with his arms outstretched to the sides as he was speaking the release of that anointing.*

PIX: *I saw a woman twirling circles as she danced before the Lord.*

HEARD: *Strongly, in culmination. Open our heaven God, open up our heaven. Crown, I've got a wife, a beautiful wife.*

WORD TO PONDER: TEARS OPENING A DOOR ABOVE YOUR HEAD 11/13/06

My fire bride, when I experience all that you have suffered to follow Me, it moves My heart to deep passion. I have never left you for a moment and I have walked with you, agonizing over you in intercession as you have adored Me in spite of it all. In the car, as you have sang your songs, we have danced upon the clouds together. On your pillow and in your tears, we have cried them in one heart. All that you do is worship and intercession. You are My fire bride, the one who is a perfect fit for Me.

My wife, My wife, My beloved wife cries over our children. Let the tears flow and let the groanings too deep to utter break open the heavens and let it rain, let it rain, let it rain. Open the floodgates of heaven and let it rain!

Hos 6:1-3 KJV
Come, and let us return unto the LORD: for he hath torn, and he will heal us; he hath smitten, and he will bind us up. After two days will he revive us: in the third day he will raise us up, and we shall live in his sight. Then shall we know, if we follow on to know the LORD: his going forth is prepared as

133

the morning; and he shall come unto us as the rain , as the latter and former rain unto the earth.

TONGUES AND THE PORTHOLE

THE DOOR OF THE PORTHOLE OPENS, THEY EAT WITH DADDY

When people receive the gift of speaking in tongues, not everyone receives in the same way. For myself, I went to kids camp in my teens and was prayed over to receive what they called the "Baptism of the Holy Spirit" (Acts 1:5) I was supposed to feel the Holy Spirit come upon me, then speak in tongues. I felt nothing when they prayed. I was expecting some bolt of lightening to come down from the sky and hit me in a whoosh of the Holy Spirit. But they simply prayed, and I simply thanked Jesus like they told me to do.

However, an hour later as I lay in my bunk bed, little foreign sounding syllables popped into my mind. So, I spoke them with my head under the pillow. It was one sentence. My counselor told me that could happen, and to be faithful to practice my new language and it would grow. So that is what I did. I spoke my one sentence faithfully for about a year! To this day, I still remember that sentence.

Then one day I was driving to school singing a popular love song along with the radio, and the second verse was sung in French. So I started singing my own pretend "French" to the words. By the end of the song, I had a complete and wonderful language, only I didn't know it! However, every time I sang that song I would sing it in my "pretend language" even when they were singing in English. It sounded so beautiful I didn't want to sing it in English. Then one day I started singing other popular love songs of the day in the same way. Then the realization hit me, I was doing

134

what the Bible called "singing in the Spirit"! (1 Corinthians 14:15) "Wow! Is this finally the expansion of my new language?" So I stopped singing and just spoke it. Sure enough, there was a full blown language!

I have received a couple of wonderful confirmations about speaking in tongues. One time I was praying in tongues and in English over people I'd met on the Internet and I saw a picture-vision of a flat bed truck driven by 2 angels. On the flat bed truck were a whole bunch of packages, each wrapped and looking exactly like the size of bricks. The Lord told me I was dispatching supplies. So I asked Him what those bricks were. He said, "Each individual prayer." Then a few days later I listened to a tape where a man was given a vision that every time he spoke in tongues, he saw packages the size of bricks come down from heaven that were deposited inside of him. When they were deposited, he felt a strengthening of his inner man. He was praying supplies for himself. So, not only did the Lord confirm that my praying in tongues was praying in supplies to others, but at the same time, I was praying in supplies for myself.

I have an interesting story about praying in supplies for others. Remember that one little sentence I mentioned when I first received tongues? When I shared it with Anna, my Mom, who also had been indoctrinated against tongues, she said it sounded like Spanish and looked it up in her Spanish dictionary. She was so surprised at the meaning, she also sought and received the Baptism of the Spirit.

Twenty-five years after that, having completely forgotten its meaning, Anna happened to ask me if I still remembered my one little sentence. I spoke what I remembered and she again looked up the words in her old Spanish dictionary, and this is what she found; my sentence was translated, "Door of a port hole released. They eat with Daddy." This was my commission from the beginning. I didn't know I was repeating a request thousands upon thousands of times. I was bombarding heaven and didn't even know it! I believe part of that fulfillment is the opened doors to a website ministry and also a writing ministry. It is a good lesson in the importance of tongues.

TONGUES: AWESOME CORPORATE AUTHORITY

Notes from a Graham Cook tape
This is a testimony from Graham Cook who is a prophet from England. He shared about one particular family in his church that was under attack. The husband and 2 sons were out of work, the wife and daughter were sick, and the husband and wife relationship was very strained. They gathered the whole congregation of 400 people into this family's house just prior to 8:00 PM. Every person that could possibly squeeze in that little home was crammed in. The only place for Graham was to sit on the toilet! The people that couldn't fit circled around the outside of the house. The instructions were that at exactly 8:00 everyone was to speak in tongues non-stop for one hour! Devils were out of there in a hurry! Repentance came, the man was instantly healed of addictions, relationships were instantly healed, both women were healed of their sickness, and the 3 guys had jobs in less than a week. Their lives were never the same. Graham said that he really believes in the commitment of "one for all and all for one." He said that if the devil kicks one family, then he has taken on the whole church.

PART THREE: AUTHORITY OF INTERCESSOR

FINDING YOUR METRON

HOW TO FIND YOUR AUTHORITY IN INTERCESSION

At a conference a few years ago, I overheard a man worshipping the Lord behind me. As he was worshipping, I heard the Lord whisper to me, "A man of authority." This of course stirred my interest and so I had to turn around and peek! I stared right into the face of a loving, prophetic intercessor (soon to be Apostle). I knew his testimony and yes he had definitely earned that title of a man of authority.

A few years ago, this powerful intercessor asked the Lord why so many intercessors were receiving spiritual backlashes and why they weren't covered. He asked the Lord this question for a long time. After unrelenting requests, the Lord finally answered him: "I will anoint My structure."

Frustrated, he said, "Lord, after my asking all this time and You didn't answer, then You finally answer, and you say THIS?" "What does THAT mean?" I laughed when I heard this, because that sounded so much like God! Through time and revelation, he understood that God would build His government, and did not want the intercessors isolated, but under the covering and protection of the Apostles and Prophets. He applied this personally by asking the prayer backing of God's chosen, when he was taking on assignments that stirred up heavy demonic forces.

In recent weeks I also have noticed that the intercessors are suffering backlash, some severely, and I have pondered the above and asked the Lord the same question: "Why is this happening?" The answer was immediate: operate within one's metron. This word metron, also has to do with God's government.

Metron comes from the scripture: "But we will not boast of things without our measure, but according to the measure (3358) of the rule which God hath distributed to us, a measure to reach even unto you." (2 Cor 10:13 KJV) Metron is a Greek word meaning: (3358) metron (met'-ron);

an apparently primary word; a measure ("metre"), literally or figuratively; by implication a limited portion (degree).

We are each given a measure of authority, and it is important to understand our metron, or sphere of influence and authority in which He has placed us. We each give (pray, stand in the gap, and war) according to our own ability. He doesn't ask us to give what we don't have, rather He asks us to give what we do have. *"If you are really eager to give, then it isn't important how much you have to give. God wants you to give what you have, not what you haven't."* *(2 Cor 8:11-12 TLB)* And therefore, it is important to understand our metron, or sphere of authority. If you are not sure what your metron is, hopefully this small outline will help kindle your thoughts to find it.

1. KNOW TO WHOM YOU ARE CALLED
Whether you are a parent, a teacher, a pastor a prophet, a public servant, etc you have a sphere of loved ones in which you have been called to nurture. If they belong to you, you have the authority to pray over what they are facing.

"And he will restore the hearts of the fathers to their children, and the hearts of the children to their fathers, lest I come and smite the land with a curse." *(Mal 4:6 NASB)*

2. KNOW YOUR GIFTS
If you don't know your calling, your giftedness can be a mirror of what your cup contains. The Lord equips whom He sends — what equipment has He given you? If you have the gift of mercy, your gift offers mercy for those deserving judgment, needing forgiveness and or needing healing. If you are a warrior and you fight demons, your gifts of discernment, hearing and seeing will reflect that function. If you have the gift of mercy and have never fought a demon in your life, God is not asking you to single-handedly tear down a strongman's demonic nest. If God has placed within you the tenacity of a bulldog to knock, knock, knock, ask, ask,

ask, then keep on making supplications! These are all gifts and He is calling you to function with what He has given you, not with what He has not.

"For as we have many members in one body, but all the members do not have the same function, so we, being many, are one body in Christ, and individually members of one another. Having then gifts differing according to the grace that is given to us, let us use them..." *(Rom 12:4-6 NKJV)*

3. KNOW YOUR ASSIGNMENTS
As an intercessor, I have been given dreams and visions of specific assignments needing completion.   I then "stand" (pray, war, hold onto His promise of victory, sacrifice, follow my conscience, etc) until it is completed. God gives each of us assignments according to our callings and when we face enemy obstacles that are a direct confrontation of completing that assignment, God gives us the authority and grace to complete it.   If you have completed that assignment, then you have also won that authority for future battles.

"His master praised him for good work. `You have been faithful in handling this small amount,' he told him, `so now I will give you many more responsibilities. Begin the joyous tasks I have assigned to you." *(Matt 25:21 TLB)*

4. KNOW YOUR MEASURE OF FAITH
We each have been given a measure of faith, and that faith can grow as He builds it via spiritual exercise. These faith muscles grow as a direct result of pressing against resistance. (When we are standing in the gap and praying, our faith directly affects the angels freedom to go forth and fight battles on our behalf.) We are called to stand, and standing takes some effort in order to resist wavering. That faith can wobble if we live a life that is not pleasing Him. Faith and favor are directly related to following our

conscience. The accuser is the first to point out the flaw and that will affect our faith to stand against onslaught. Our metron will be no larger than our faith to be able to stand in His favor.

"For through the grace given to me I say to every man among you not to think more highly of himself than he ought to think; but to think so as to have sound judgment, as God has allotted to each a measure of faith." (Rom 12:3 NASB)

"Therefore the children of Israel could not stand before their enemies, but turned their backs before their enemies, because they have become doomed to destruction. Neither will I be with you anymore, unless you destroy the accursed from among you. Get up, sanctify the people, and say, 'Sanctify yourselves for tomorrow, because thus says the LORD God of Israel: "There is an accursed thing in your midst, O Israel; you cannot stand before your enemies until you take away the accursed thing from among you." (Josh 7:12-13 NKJV)

5. KNOW YOUR PATTERN OF SUCCESSES

When entering into new territory, the Lord will build your faith with confirmations, to help you to understand His approval of your moving ahead in prayer. If you can look back and find a link of similar prayer successes, this will be a good indicator of your metron. We have a fellow at our church who began getting Words of knowledge of prayer needs. He took courage and started sharing what he believed the Lord was saying. Each time he did this, someone responded and he prayed for them. Each time they received answers to the prayers. This is a good indicator through a pattern of success, that he has been given a metron to pray for those whom he receives Words of knowledge.

"I will drive them out before you little by little, until you become fruitful and take possession of the land." (Ex 23:30 NASB)

6. KNOW YOUR OPPONENT

It is true that your greatest gifting (and or promise) will also be your greatest testing. Sometimes if you are suffering a backlash it is because the devil considers you a threat and he knows you are influencing his domain. If that is the case, be encouraged that you are making a difference.

"Then Jesus, full of the Holy Spirit, left the Jordan River, being urged by the Spirit out into the barren wastelands of Judea, where Satan tempted him for forty days. (Luke 4:1 TLB)

7. KNOW REVELATION

The Lord will send you supernatural revelations of your portion. This comes through the many ways to hear Him and they puzzle together to give a good indicator of your sphere of influence. Ask Him for revelation to teach you your metron.

"But the anointing which you have received from Him abides in you, and you do not need that anyone teach you; but as the same anointing teaches you concerning all things, and is true, and is not a lie, and just as it has taught you, you will abide in Him." (1 John 2:27 NKJV)

8. KNOW YOUR COVERING

God is raising up His government, and He is divinely moving His chosen leaders into place. If the leaders are saying to pray corporately against a demonic problem, then that is the covering and guidance in which to safely operate your gifts. Corporately means standing in one accord with other believers against a common cause. There is a synergistic effect when joining with others of likemindedness to fight a common enemy.

"You will chase your enemies, and they shall fall by the sword before you. Five of you shall chase a hundred, and a

hundred of you shall put ten thousand to flight." (Lev 26:7-8 NKJV)

I close with a precious forwarded story that has a 2 fold theme. It reflects the heart of any true covering appointed by God, and it also reflects the Lord's heart to us all:

"A mother took her 8 year old son to a great concert hall, black tie event to hear Paderewski the famous composer-pianist. The boy became restless waiting for the concert to start so as his mother visited with friends he slipped from her side and onto the stage. He was drawn by the Steinway and climbed up on the stool and stared wide-eyed at the keys. He placed his small trembling fingers in the right location and began to play "Chopsticks."   The roar of the crowd was hushed as hundreds of frowning faces turned in his direction. Irritated and embarrassed, they began to shout: "Get that boy away from there. "Who'd bring a kid that young in here?" "Where's his mother?" "Somebody stop him!"

Backstage the master overheard the sounds out in front and quickly put together in his mind what was happening. Hurriedly, he grabbed his coat and rushed toward the stage. Without one word of announcement he stooped over behind the boy, reached around both sides, and began to improvise a counter melody to harmonize and enhance "chopsticks". As the two played together, Paderewski kept whispering in the boy's ear: "Keep going, don't quit, son. keep on playing.. don't stop....don't quit."

And so it is with us. We hammer away on our project, which seems about as significant as "Chopsticks" in a concert hall. And about the time we are ready to give up, along comes the Master, who leans over and whispers: "Now keep going; don't quit. Keep on...don't stop , don't quit!"

THE POWER OF HIS WORD

RHEMA 2/27/07 WHERE YOU WALK THE GROUND SHAKES

HEARD: *Heaven. Grounded. We see you, all of us. The full potential. Where you walk, the ground shakes.*

Isa 66:5 NKJV
Hear the word of the LORD, you who tremble at His word.

Heb 12:25-29 NKJV
See that you do not refuse Him who speaks. For if they did not escape who refused Him who spoke on earth, much more shall we not escape if we turn away from Him who speaks from heaven, 26 whose voice then shook the earth; but now He has promised, saying, "Yet once more I shake not only the earth, but also heaven." 27 Now this, "Yet once more," indicates the removal of those things that are being shaken, as of things that are made, that the things which cannot be shaken may remain.

Therefore, since we are receiving a kingdom which cannot be shaken, let us have grace, by which we may serve God acceptably with reverence and godly fear. 29 For our God is a consuming fire.

COMMENTS: If the prophetic truly understood the full potential of the power and reverberations when releasing God's Word, they would season it with greater temperance and much mercy. And if they understood why God tells them secrets, they would salt their sacrifices to God asking that He stay His hand. God is asking for intercessors to stand in the cracks.

Gen 18:17-21 NKJV
And the LORD said, "Shall I hide from Abraham what I am doing, since Abraham shall surely become a great and mighty nation, and all the nations of the earth shall be blessed in him? For I have known him, in order that he may command his children and his household after him, that they

143

keep the way of the LORD, to do righteousness and justice, that the LORD may bring to Abraham what He has spoken to him." And the LORD said, "Because the outcry against Sodom and Gomorrah is great, and because their sin is very grave, I will go down now and see whether they have done altogether according to the outcry against it that has come to Me; and if not, I will know."

Matt 5:13 NKJV
"You are the salt of the earth; but if the salt loses its flavor, how shall it be seasoned? It is then good for nothing but to be thrown out and trampled underfoot by men.

Isa 59:19 NKJV
Then the LORD saw it, and it displeased Him That there was no justice. 16 He saw that there was no man, And wondered that there was no intercessor ;Therefore His own arm brought salvation for Him; And His own righteousness, it sustained Him. 17 For He put on righteousness as a breastplate, And a helmet of salvation on His head ;He put on the garments of vengeance for clothing, And was clad with zeal as a cloak. 18 According to their deeds, accordingly He will repay, Fury to His adversaries, Recompense to His enemies; The coastlands He will fully repay. 19 So shall they fear The name of the LORD from the west, And His glory from the rising of the sun; When the enemy comes in like a flood, The Spirit of the LORD will lift up a standard against him.

WHAT WILL YOU DECREE?

HEARD SONG [6/25/05]: *Pull out the red carpet. What will you decree?*

HEARD: *Victory. Measuring stick. Rule. My wife. Penetrate with revelation. The metron she's been given. Yes we're together. Peace. Link.*

HEARD {as I was thinking about the word decree}: *Edict.*

WORD STUDY: TO DECREE

Job 22:28-30 AMP
You shall also decide and decree [1504] a thing, and it shall be established for you; and the light [of God's favor] shall shine upon your ways. When they make [you] low, you will say, [There is] a lifting up; and the humble person He lifts up and saves. He will even deliver the one [for whom you intercede] who is not innocent; yes, he will be delivered through the cleanness of your hands. [Job 42:7,8.]

OT:1504
OT:1504 gazar (gaw-zar'); a primitive root; to cut down or off; (figuratively) to destroy, divide, exclude, or decide: KJV - cut down (off), decree, divide, snatch.

Ps 2:7-12 NKJV
"I will declare the decree: The LORD has said to Me, 'You are My Son, Today I have begotten You. Ask of Me, and I will give You The nations for Your inheritance, And the ends of the earth for Your possession. You shall break them with a rod of iron; You shall dash them to pieces like a potter's vessel.'" Now therefore, be wise, O kings; Be instructed, you judges of the earth. Serve the LORD with fear, And rejoice with trembling. Kiss the Son, lest He be angry, And you perish in the way, When His wrath is kindled but a little. Blessed are all those who put their trust in Him.

Ps 148:5-6 NKJV
Let them praise the name of the LORD, For He commanded and they were created. He also established them forever and ever; He made a decree which shall not pass away.

Ezra 5:13 KJV
But in the first year of Cyrus the king of Babylon the same king Cyrus made a decree [2942] to build this house of God.

te`em

OT:2942 te`em (Aramaic) (teh-ame'); from OT:2939, and equivalent to OT:294 l; properly, flavor; figuratively, judgment (both subjective and objective); hence, account (both subj. and obj.):
KJV - chancellor, command, commandment, decree, regard, taste, wisdom.

CONFIRMATION: Today after writing the below Word to Ponder on decreeing, I turned with anointed hands to the following paragraph in one of my ponder books:

I AM calling you to also release your own seeds of intercession and declaration over America and over the world. I have anointed you with great power of influence. For such a time as this, it is time to release that power and anointing through prayer and declaration. You have a host of angels that are waiting to be released as you speak forth My kingdom on earth, even as I have declared it in heaven.

WORD TO PONDER: STEP FORWARD INTO YOUR AUTHORITY
When I ask you to step forward into your authority, it is like taking one step onto the red carpet. A line of spiritual favor and honor has been rolled out before you. As you step forward into that place, there is a pathway paved before you. It is a safe place lined with My blood. I have placed My life and My Name on this line. All that you decree follows that bloodline and even sets your progeny free. Speak and declare My freedom over all that I reveal to you, My dear one.

Job 22:28 AMP

You shall also decide and decree a thing, and it shall be established for you; and the light [of God's favor] shall shine upon your ways.

Est 8:8 NLT
Now go ahead and send a message to the Jews in the king's name, telling them whatever you want, and seal it with the king's signet ring. But remember that whatever is written in the king's name and sealed with his ring can never be revoked."

STAND BOLDLY AND DECLARE HIS WORD

RHEMA 1/21/99: When I got back from home group I heard the Lord speak to me.

HEARD: *Model prayer.*

I has been feeling condemned for praying over someone at home group, as I wasn't sure if I offended him or not. He was worried about a lump on his body being cancer. I took authority over it and cursed the seed of cancer in Jesus Name and also cut the seed of cancer from being passed onto him from his blood line.

RELIEF UPDATE: His wife told me the following week that they really appreciated the prayer as his Dad had died of cancer, which I didnt know. This week he was able to go to the doctor and the lump ended up being fat!

Mark 11:20-24 NKJV
Now in the morning, as they passed by, they saw the fig tree dried up from the roots. 21 And Peter, remembering, said to Him, "Rabbi, look! The fig tree which You cursed has withered away." So Jesus answered and said to them, "Have faith in God. 23 For assuredly, I say to you, whoever says to this mountain, 'Be removed and be cast into the sea,' and does not doubt in his heart, but believes that those things he says will be done, he will have whatever he says.

INTERCESSORS BATTLE STRONGHOLDS IN MINDSETS

INTERCESSORS WINNING A WAR WITH WORDS

As intercessors battling mind-sets, sometimes it take years of spending one word at a time. And when these words are falling upon the hearts of the blinded ones we love, we sometimes get wounded because they kick back with a strong wallop.

As intercessors sometimes it is very hard to distinguish between battling demons and mind-sets of men. I have battled both and believe that stubborn and blinded mind-sets are by far the worst opponent. And this is what Jesus fought in the blindedness of the religious of His day. We never saw Jesus model how to directly fight principalities behind the religious thinking of His day, rather He used the weapon of Words upon the mindsets of people. Those who were called and drawn by His Spirit, heard Him and changed their ways of thinking.

2 Cor 10:1-6 NKJV
Now I, Paul, myself am pleading with you by the meekness and gentleness of Christ — who in presence am lowly among you, but being absent am bold toward you. 2 But I beg you that when I am present I may not be bold with that confidence by which I intend to be bold against some, who think of us as if we walked according to the flesh. 3 For though we walk in the flesh, we do not war according to the flesh. 4 For the weapons of our warfare are not carnal but mighty in God for pulling down strongholds, 5 casting down arguments and every high thing that exalts itself against the knowledge of God, bringing every thought into captivity to the obedience of Christ, 6 and being ready to punish all disobedience when your obedience is fulfilled.

THE INFRASTRUCTURE OF WINNING A WAR WITH WORDS

QUICKENED SIGN: *Honoring ordinary people who do extraordinary things.*

QUICKENED MOVIE: Today we went to the movie, Amazing Grace. I heard the Word of the Lord through William Wilberforce's life. He felt called by God and didn't know how to resolve that and his desire for parliament. As it worked out He served God in parliament. Near the beginning of the movie I heard the Lord say "A war with words" and then watched as William spent the passion of his youth and health in unrelenting, persevering conviction to work on the mindsets of his peers through his words. From one man against all, he finally turned abolition of slavery to the popular vote and ended the slave trade in Great Britain.

I felt a deep undercurrent of God's heartbeat in the fact that He is using His servants to win a war with Words. Instead of directly battling principalities and demons, they are sent to destroy strongholds built through mindsets. As for me, He is doing it all with the whisp of a feather pen. Wayne once saw me on a white horse and my weapon was a huge white feathered pen that touched the ground and swept up over my shoulder. (smile) Only God can do such a thing with a feather! I have long believed that it is much easier to cast out demons than to touch the mindsets of free willed men.

It was interesting to me that at the end of the movie one of the members of parliament stood to his feet to honor William, who had spent so much to win the minds and votes of those whose wealth depended upon the slave trade. He said something to the fact that Napoleon was a great man who won a great war, but when it was all over he had the haunting memories of dead men. But William, a common man won his war through peace and returned home to sleep in peace. The Holy Spirit immediately brought back the quickened poster I read before I went into the movie: "Honoring ordinary people who do extraordinary things." And thus, the power of spending one Word at a time, daring to topple strongholds while trusting God to empower mere pennies and feathers.

2 Cor 10:3-6 NKJV
For though we walk in the flesh, we do not war according to the flesh. For the weapons of our warfare are not carnal but mighty in God for pulling down strongholds , casting down arguments and every high thing that exalts itself against the knowledge of God, bringing every thought into captivity to the obedience of Christ, and being ready to punish all disobedience when your obedience is fulfilled.

THE INVESTMENT OF AN INFRASTRUCTURE
I was touched by the fact that in the movie, William was a student of John Newton who had been a slave trader and then came to the Lord in repentance. John was the one who wrote the song, Amazing Grace. It was John's influence that seeded and fueled William's passion. As I thought of the power of mentoring, to pour one's life into another, I saw the power of what it means to be a bridge...the infrastructure that moves people to commitment.

When Wayne and I were still young and I went back to college to finish my degree, I did my thesis and research on opening a store in a local mall. After all the facts were gathered, we chose not to open a store in the brand new mall that was being built at the time. We realized that the first business of its kind is the one who spends most of their money to change the mindsets of the people, and actually build the infrastructure. If they have a new product or new idea, they have to convince the public of its benefit. After that business has spent everything on its dream, it is actually the second business that comes in with the identical product that becomes the success. It reaps all the previous advertising that went into convincing the public of its need. This truth has been played out in many arenas of life.

We saw this on a practical level where the mall contract required the businesses to finish the inside of their store.

When you walked into the spaces for lease, they were actually bare infrastructure without walls, fixtures or anything. It was a minimum of a $25,000 before even starting that had to be freely left behind for the next store in line. Back then, that was a lot of money.

Today as I was thinking about the slave trader who repented and told his story to young William, I saw him as a parable of today's bridge.... A generation that takes the time to mentor and invest in our kids. There is so much life spent in building an infrastructure, and once built it is rarely seen or its details understood. But what remains is the passion to move the harvest of what was invested of time, energy and commitment to the finish line. Our harvest and our inheritance IS our children. And that is why God said that infrastructures of those who planted in our lives could not become perfect without us.

So the slave trader repented and told his story to one who listened. And the one who listened took a torch and changed nations.

Heb 11:40 AMP
Because God had us in mind and had something better and greater in view for us, so that they [these heroes and heroines of faith] should not come to perfection apart from us [before we could join them].

QUICKENED AD: When we walked out of the movie and down this same mall, we stopped at the food court to get a bite to eat. My eye glanced at an advertisement: "Purchasing millions with just pennies." I looked away and smiled, thinking of "one sent" (cent) and the simple power of spending a penny, one Word at a time. Yes there are many ways to win a war, but it is the God of peace that crushes the enemy under foot. And He does so with a war of Words.

Ps 33:6-9 NKJV

By the word of the LORD the heavens were made, and all the host of them by the breath of His mouth. He gathers the waters of the sea together as a heap;

He lays up the deep in storehouses. Let all the earth fear the LORD; Let all the inhabitants of the world stand in awe of Him. For He spoke, and it was done;
He commanded, and it stood fast.

Rev 12:10-11 m NKJV
Then I heard a loud voice saying in heaven, "Now salvation, and strength, and the kingdom of our God, and the power of His Christ have come, for the accuser of our brethren, who accused them before our God day and night, has been cast down. And they overcame him by the blood of the Lamb and by the word of their testimony , and they did not love their lives to the death.

Luke 21:14-16 NKJV
Therefore settle it in your hearts not to meditate beforehand on what you will answer; for I will give you a mouth and wisdom which all your adversaries will not be able to contradict or resist.

RESTORING THE DOORKEEPER

TEACHING: The following revelation is about restoring the calling and authority of being a doorkeeper. Within every family, church, school, job, community, region, etc there are prescribed boundaries of authority that govern each group. This is true in the natural and true in the spiritual. Within groups, every one of us have authority and the power to cast our vote in the area in which we have responsibility to plant our time, our prayers, our callings, our gifts and our assigned positions. Even if we are a child taking care of a beloved pet, we can open and close doors on behalf of protecting such!

After I received the rhema in this post about His restoring this post of doorkeeper, He told me an area where He wanted me to make a decision about either opening or closing the door. I had been hearing the term stalemate recently and He told me that in the spirit there was a stalemate. As a doorkeeper, I had been given the swing vote and that I needed to wait upon Him for as much input as possible because my one vote could literally swing the door open or close in this situation! I was astounded and realized it was like being a judge with a gavel and having the power to say Yes or No. This put the fear of God in me! But I knew this was truth.

And now here is the revelation as it was given to me:

RHEMA 9/23/06 CASTING YOUR VOTE AS A DOORKEEPER

VISION: *I saw some property that had been staked out. The corner stake was missing on one of the 4 sides. The stake was to establish the boundaries and had previously been planted in the exact corner. I could see that the hole for the stake was still there but now the ground level had sunk at the corner, and so it had fallen and needed re-staking.*

The Lord revealed to me in viewing it that it was a position that had fallen and needed to be restored. The ground level needed to be built up and firmly established again so the stake could again be secured. In spiritual terms, this is "taking territory that had fallen down. It is also rebuilding that which had fallen."

HEARD: *I'm in need of you. The whole hosts. We all are. How about we do this together? We're going into new places. Door open, you left a door open. Swing vote. This swing vote needs to be a very careful decision. It represents too much. What time is it?*

CLOCK TIME: 7:55

[7 = Completion; 5 = double portion grace. Time to close the door to the old season, and come into the new one of grace, grace.]

[I then pondered and prayed about the decision of either closing or leaving the door open to an area He had been speaking to me about.]

CONFIRMATION QUICKENED SONG: Immediately after, I turned on my IPOD and shuffled the 300+ songs. The song came on, I would rather be a doorkeeper in the house of My God, then to dwell in the tents of the wicked. This song was a home recording of someone's worship and the only words in the whole song was that phrase!!! She sang it over and over and over again. Talk about confirmation!

That song comes from the following scripture:

SCRIPTURES ABOUT DOORKEEPER

Ps 84:12 NKJV
How lovely is Your tabernacle, O LORD of hosts! My soul longs, yes, even faints For the courts of the LORD; My heart and my flesh cry out for the living God. Even the sparrow has found a home, And the swallow a nest for herself, Where she may lay her young — Even Your altars, O LORD of hosts, My King and my God. Blessed are those who dwell in Your house; They will still be praising You. Selah Blessed is the man whose strength is in You, Whose heart is set on pilgrimage. As they pass through the Valley of Baca, They make it a spring; The rain also covers it with pools. They go from strength to strength; Each one appears before God in Zion. O LORD God of hosts, hear my prayer; Give ear, O God of Jacob! Selah O God, behold our shield, And look upon the face of Your anointed. FOR A DAY IN YOUR COURTS IS BETTER THAN A THOUSAND. I WOULD RATHER BE A DOORKEEPER IN THE HOUSE OF MY GOD THAN DWELL IN THE TENTS OF WICKEDNESS. For the LORD God is a sun and shield; The LORD will give grace and glory; No good thing will He withhold From those

who walk uprightly. O LORD of hosts, Blessed is the man who trusts in You!

QUICKENED REVELATION: Suddenly I realized two things about that scripture I had never seen before:

For a day in Your courts is better than a thousand. I would rather be a doorkeeper in the house of my God than dwell in the tents of wickedness.

1. To be a doorkeeper is like being in a COURT room of decision.

2. If you dwell in the tent of the wicked you don't have the authority to cast your vote for anything but wickedness.

CONFIRMATION QUICKENED GESTURE: I turned on my computer to type in my rhema, and the screen popped on that said, WELCOME. I found my mouse finger drawing a circle around the word Welcome. I have never done that before and it was an absentminded pass time while I was waiting. Suddenly the Lord opened my eyes that it was a prophetic gesture because the term, "Welcome" is the phrase used to open a door! I was drawing circles around this word.

CONFIRMATION: When the computer was finally on (smile) I downloaded my emails. And the report came through of those who had un-subscribed to my email list. There were 2 addresses on it and one email address had the word "doorkeeper" in it!!! I saw that not only was that a confirmation to being a door keeper and casting our votes, but they had closed a door to receiving from this ministry.

He had my thorough attention!!! It is time to become doorkeepers and cast our votes in the areas in which He has given us authority.

UPDATE CONFIRMATION 9/24/06 I turned with anointed hands this morning to a new place I had never seen before. I highlighted the following in my Bible that I placed in all caps below. It was very revealing to me to notice that they had gatekeepers established on all 4 sides, and that was exactly what I had seen in the vision of the property with the stake missing, - that the property had 4 sides.

1 Chron 9:17-27 NLT
The gatekeepers who returned were Shallum, Akkub, Talmon, Ahiman, and their relatives. Shallum was the chief gatekeeper . Prior to this time, they were **RESPONSIBLE FOR THE KING'S GATE** on the east side. These men served as gatekeepers for the camps of the Levites. Shallum was the son of Kore, a descendant of Abiasaph, from the clan of Korah. He and his relatives, the Korahites, were **RESPONSIBLE FOR GUARDING THE ENTRANCE TO THE SANCTUARY**, just as their ancestors had guarded the Tabernacle in the camp of the LORD. Phinehas son of Eleazar had been in charge of the gatekeepers in earlier times, and the LORD had been with him. And later Zechariah son of Meshelemiah had been responsible for guarding the entrance to the Tabernacle.

In all, there were 212 gatekeepers in those days, and they were listed by genealogies in their villages. David and Samuel the seer had appointed their ancestors because they were **RELIABLE MEN**. These gatekeepers and their descendants, by their divisions, were **RESPONSIBLE FOR GUARDING THE ENTRANCE** to the house of the LORD, the house that was formerly a tent. The gatekeepers were **STATIONED ON ALL FOUR SIDES** — east, west, north, and south. From time to time, their relatives in the villages came to share their duties for seven-day periods.

The four chief gatekeepers, all Levites, were **IN AN OFFICE OF GREAT TRUST**, for they were **RESPONSIBLE FOR THE ROOMS AND TREASURIES AT THE HOUSE OF GOD**. They would spend the night around the house of God, since it was their **DUTY TO GUARD IT**. It was also their **JOB TO OPEN THE GATES EVERY MORNING**.

OTHER SCRIPTURES WITH THE WORD DOOR KEEPER

- ## THEY REPAIRED THE DOORS

2 Chron 29:3-7 NLKV
*In the first year of his reign, in the first month, he **OPENED THE DOORS OF THE HOUSE OF THE LORD AND REPAIRED THEM**. 4 Then he brought in the priests and the Levites, and gathered them in the East Square, 5 and said to them: "Hear me, Levites! Now sanctify yourselves, sanctify the house of the LORD God of your fathers, and carry out the rubbish from the holy place. 6 For our fathers have trespassed and done evil in the eyes of the LORD our God; they have forsaken Him, have turned their faces away from the dwelling place of the LORD, and turned their backs on Him. 7 They have also shut up the doors of the vestibule, put out the lamps, and have not burned incense or offered burnt offerings in the holy place to the God of Israel.*

- ## DOORS REPRESENT BOUNDARIES

Job 38:8-11 NKJV
"Or who shut in the sea with doors, When it burst forth and issued from the womb; 9 When I made the clouds its garment, And thick darkness its swaddling band; 10 When I fixed My limit for it, And set bars and doors ; 11 When I said,'This far you may come, but no farther, And here your proud waves must stop!'

- ## DOORS THAT OPEN TO SEE HIS FACE ARE WITHOUT IDOLS

Ps 24:3-10 NKJV
Who may ascend into the hill of the LORD? or who may stand in His holy place? 4 He who has clean hands and a pure heart, WHO HAS NOT LIFTED UP HIS SOUL TO AN IDOL, or sworn deceitfully. 5 He shall receive blessing from the LORD ,And righteousness from the God of his salvation.

6 This is Jacob, the generation of those who seek Him, Who seek Your face. Selah

Lift up your heads, O you gates! And be lifted up, you everlasting doors! And the King of glory shall come in. 8 Who is this King of glory? The LORD strong and mighty, The LORD mighty in battle. 9 Lift up your heads, O you gates! LIFT UP, YOU EVERLASTING DOORS !AND THE KING OF GLORY SHALL COME IN. 10 Who is this King of glory? The LORD of hosts, He is the King of glory.

- CYRUS THE DOOR KEEPER

Isa 45:6 NKJV
"Thus says the LORD to His anointed, To Cyrus, whose right hand I have held — To subdue nations before him And loose the armor of kings, TO OPEN BEFORE HIM THE DOUBLE DOORS,SO THAT THE GATES WILL NOT BE SHUT: 2'I will go before you And make the crooked places straight; I will break in pieces the gates of bronze And cut the bars of iron. 3 I will give you the treasures of darkness And hidden riches of secret places, That you may know that I, the LORD, Who call you by your name, Am the God of Israel. 4 For Jacob My servant's sake, And Israel My elect, I have even called you by your name; I have named you, though you have not known Me. 5 I am the LORD, and there is no other; There is no God besides Me. I will gird you, though you have not known Me, 6 That they may know from the rising of the sun to its setting That there is none besides Me.

- THE GOVERNMENT OF DAVID OPENS AND CLOSES DOORS

Isa 22:22-23 NKJV
The key of the house of David I will lay on his shoulder; So he shall open, and no one shall shut; And he shall shut, and no one shall open. 23 I will fasten him as a peg in a secure place, And he will become a glorious throne to his father's house.

Rev 3:7-12 NKJV
"And to the angel of the church in Philadelphia write, 'These things says He who is holy, He who is true, "He who has the key of David, He who opens and no one shuts, and shuts and no one opens": 8 "I know your works. See, I have set before you an open door, and no one can shut it; for you have a little strength, have kept My word, and have not denied My name. 9 Indeed I will make those of the synagogue of Satan, who say they are Jews and are not, but lie — indeed I will make them come and worship before your feet, and to know that I have loved you. 10 Because you have kept My command to persevere, I also will keep you from the hour of trial which shall come upon the whole world, to test those who dwell on the earth. 11 Behold, I am coming quickly! Hold fast what you have, that no one may take your crown. 12 He who overcomes, I will make him a pillar in the temple of My God, and he shall go out no more. I will write on him the name of My God and the name of the city of My God, the New Jerusalem, which comes down out of heaven from My God. And I will write on him My new name.

- THE WATCHMAN KEEPS THE DOORS

Mark 13:33-37 NKJV
Take heed, watch and pray; for you do not know when the time is. 34 It is like a man going to a far country, who left his house and gave authority to his servants, and to each his work, and commanded the doorkeeper to watch. 35 Watch therefore, for you do not know when the master of the house is coming — in the evening, at midnight, at the crowing of the rooster, or in the morning — 36 lest, coming suddenly, he find you sleeping. 37 And what I say to you, I say to all: Watch!"

- DISCERNMENT OF WHO & WHAT YOU HEAR OPENS AND CLOSES DOORS

John 10:1-6 NKJV
"Most assuredly, I say to you, he who does not enter the sheepfold by the door, but climbs up some other way, the

same is a thief and a robber. 2 But he who enters by the door is the shepherd of the sheep. 3 To him the doorkeeper opens, and the sheep hear his voice; and he calls his own sheep by name and leads them out. 4 And when he brings out his own sheep, he goes before them; and the sheep follow him, for they know his voice. 5 Yet they will by no means follow a stranger, but will flee from him, for they do not know the voice of strangers." 6 Jesus used this illustration, but they did not understand the things which He spoke to them.

WORD TO PONDER: RESTORING THE AUTHORITY OF THE DOORKEEPER 9/23/06

I AM restoring the authority of the doorkeeper. Within every family, church, school, job, community, region, there are prescribed boundaries of authority that govern in the natural and in the spiritual. The doorkeepers have the authority and power to cast votes in areas where they have planted their time, prayers, callings, gifts and assigned positions.

These doorkeepers are given the authority to say yes or no. Such a position has the power to break spiritual stalemates; the swing vote where the one vote will turn the tide of destiny. In stalemates, this is operating as a judge in the spiritual realm, with the power of the gavel to establish the boundaries of finality.

Walk with clean hands, a pure heart with a soul cleansed from idolatry. Do not abide with the wicked. Do not make your decisions in presumption or haste. Judge nothing before its time, but instead wait upon Me to bring the revelations needed to cast a righteous vote. Be responsible and reliable to guard the doors of those you care for, and close the door against the wolf that seeks to tear and rip asunder.

PS 84:12 NKJV
For a day in Your courts is better than a thousand. I would rather be a doorkeeper in the house of my God Than dwell in the tents of wickedness. For the LORD God is a sun and shield; The LORD will give grace and glory; No good thing will He withhold From those who walk uprightly. O LORD of hosts, Blessed is the man who trusts in You!

Isa 22:22-23 NKJV
The key of the house of David I will lay on his shoulder; So he shall open, and no one shall shut; And he shall shut, and no one shall open. 23 I will fasten him as a peg in a secure place, And he will become a glorious throne to his father's house.

INHERITANCE OF RULING AND REIGNING

COMMENTS: God has given us the inheritance of stepping into divine rule. It was His intent and purpose that we would have dominion over the earth.

Jesus clearly said it was not His will to kill, steal or destroy, but to give life. We were given the earth to nurture and take care of it. In the book of Revelations it says that He will judge those who hurt the earth.

The earth was placed under the bondage of decay and corruption due to sin. And when God's children step into their places of divine rule and reign, they will set the earth back into harmony with heaven by releasing it to praise and glorify God. They will release the earth to praise the Lord by binding the demonic plans on the earth, cursing its fruit, and in the opposite spirit, loosing God's redemptive plan in its stead and planting the fruit of righteousness to take its place. They will do this for whatever demonic plan and fruit they see that is not giving glory to God upon the earth.

Ps 115:16 NKJV

The heaven, even the heavens, are the LORD's; But the earth He has given to the children of men.

Ps 8:4-6 NKJV
What is man that You are mindful of him, and the son of man that You visit him? For You have made him a little lower than the angels, and You have crowned him with glory and honor. You have made him to have dominion over the works of Your hands; You have put all things under his feet,

John 10:10 NKJV
The thief does not come except to steal, and to kill, and to destroy. I have come that they may have life , and that they may have it more abundantly.

Rev 11:17-18 NKJV
"We give You thanks, O Lord God Almighty, the One who is and who was and who is to come, because You have taken Your great power and reigned. The nations were angry, and Your wrath has come, and the time of the dead, that they should be judged, and that You should reward Your servants the prophets and the saints, and those who fear Your name, small and great, and should destroy those who destroy the earth."

Rom 8:19-22 NKJV
For the earnest expectation of the creation eagerly waits for the revealing of the sons of God. For the creation was subjected to futility, not willingly, but because of Him who subjected it in hope; because the creation itself also will be delivered from the bondage of corruption into the glorious liberty of the children of God. For we know that the whole creation groans and labors with birth pangs together until now.

Matt 6:9-10 NKJV
Our Father in heaven, hallowed be Your name. Your kingdom come. Your will be done on earth as it is in heaven.

Matt 16:17-19 NKJV

"Blessed are you, Simon Bar-Jonah, for flesh and blood has not revealed this to you, but My Father who is in heaven. 18 And I also say to you that you are Peter, and on this rock I will build My church, and the gates of Hades shall not prevail against it. 19 And I will give you the keys of the kingdom of heaven, and whatever you bind on earth will be bound in heaven, and whatever you loose on earth will be loosed in heaven."

AUTHORITY OVER WEATHER

INTERESTING TRAINING 1/13/98: Today I was very busy organizing closets. Suddenly I heard a huge gust of wind and the chairs on our back porch tipped over and made a clatter. I looked and barely saw the wind blowing. It started to rain heavily and I went back to work.

Then about 15 times I kept hearing the phrase, "A propensity towards evil." At first I wondered what propensity meant, then I realized it meant inclination. I wondered if my thought life was OK, then checked to see if I had been TA some person who might have this inclination, and who needed prayer. Often I hear people's names and pray for them on the spot. I came up with nothing I could think of. Then I kept hearing this phrase. Finally I started rebuking it as a pestering spirit. It kept on. Then suddenly I heard a blast of wind again.

I then wondered if what I was hearing was the Lord warning me to pray about the weather. Instead of really taking it seriously, I bound the enemy and said, "May this wind cause no harm in Jesus Name." It was spoken like a benediction instead of a command. I promptly forgot about it because I stopped hearing the phrase. Later I was thinking about the wind, and heard the enemy say, "We're very angry with you." I said, "Of course you are!" and rebuked it and commanded it to shut up in Jesus Name and went back to work.

That evening I watched the local news. They were interviewing a telephone wire man who said, "What it was, was a hurricane. The hurricane lasted about 20 seconds and left!"

The pictures showed a huge tree down across a major traffic street. The man had been across the street and had witnessed the tree falling and was really grateful he wasn't hurt. Also 1,000 residents had no power in another place that had lost several trees. I suddenly realized what my day was about. I was grateful no one was hurt, but felt like I could have done more if I had prayed more seriously. I haven't yet swallowed that the Lord is training me to take authority over weather issues and teaching me small chunks at a time. I am convinced that there is a propensity towards an evil spirit to use every tornado, hurricane and flood. It is much more than natural events occurring.

Last year we had at least 2 tornadoes strike our area that simply does not have tornadoes. They both had a small path of destruction within city limits. I felt at the time both of them were brought on by evil spirits.

UPDATE CONFIRMATION: I read in Bob Jones Shepherd's rod shortly after this: "The intercessors were told in this year's Day of Atonement revelation to file charges against mother nature. When Jesus and His disciples were crossing the sea of Galilee, a storm empowered with demonic forces attempted to withstand them as they crossed. The Lord stood in the boat and rebuked the storm. He removed the evil power causing the storm, bringing a calm to the Sea of Galilee. In the same way, the intercessors are going to have to stand in the authority of God's Word and rebuke the demonic forces that are empowering many of the devastating storms that are coming to the earth. When these storms begin to approach, the intercessors must stand to rebuke the storms and turn them away. Believers are given the authority to deal with these storms. The amount of damage done by the coming natural disasters will greatly depend upon the willingness of the church to intercede and combat these forces on behalf of mankind."

HEARD the enemy say: *Authority. We're out of here.*

WORD TO PONDER TRAINING FOR AUTHORITY OVER THE ELEMENTS 1/13/98

I am training my intercessors to understand the elements. The wind and the rain and all the elements of weather are governed by My natural laws that I have set in motion. However behind each and every element is a propensity towards evil. The demonic forces take advantage of some weather patterns to bring sudden and unexpected havoc and destruction. Use this understanding to bind any evil forces behind the wind, the rain and the elements. Loose protection over your area. You will be surprised that even the most simple of prayers over what you see with your own eyes, will wipe out evil plans even miles away.

"And he arose, and rebuked the wind, and said unto the sea, Peace, be still. And the wind ceased, and there was a great calm." (Mark 4:39 KJV)

PIX 1/22/98: *I saw a blast of wind blowing the enemy army away.*

HEARD: *Jet stream. Your city. God will place a wall or hedge around it for your sake.*

Ps 35:4-6 NKJV
Let those be put to shame and brought to dishonor who seek after my life; Let those be turned back and brought to confusion who plot my hurt. Let them be like chaff before the wind, and let the angel of the LORD chase them. Let their

way be dark and slippery, and let the angel of the LORD pursue them.

WORD TO PONDER JET STREAM PROTECTION 1/22/98
When you need it, I will blow a blast of My breath into the jet stream. It shall carry the enemy's intentions away from your city. For I have placed a wall and a hedge around it for your sake.

"So Moses lifted his hand toward heaven, and there was deep darkness over the entire land for three days. 23 During all that time the people scarcely moved, for they could not see. But there was light as usual where the people of Israel lived." (Ex 10:22-23 NLT)

USE YOUR AUTHORITY OVER CREATION

HEARD 6/15/07: *Second chance. Bird flu. Pandemic. Watch your step. Make the right choice. Live. Ruling and reigning, it's a must. Use your authority, take your rod.*

DECLARATION: Lord, we speak forth life, and health and blessing upon the birds - the fowls of the air... And we declare they are good. We release them from the curse of plague and loose them to life. We release them to live and not die...to be blessed and not cursed.

Lord we ask that You will put a stop to the bird flu and place a boundary that it not passover to humans. We ask for Your mercy to cover our sins and set us free from the demonic plans of death and destruction, in Jesus Name. We ask that You will draw Your people to repent, pray and begin to make positive decrees over our world.

Gen 1:20-23 NKJV
Then God said, "Let the waters abound with an abundance of living creatures, and let birds fly above the earth across

the face of the firmament of the heavens." 21 So God created great sea creatures and every living thing that moves, with which the waters abounded, according to their kind, and every winged bird according to its kind. And God saw that it was good. 22 And God blessed them, saying,"Be fruitful and multiply, and fill the waters in the seas, and let birds multiply on the earth." 23 So the evening and the morning were the fifth day.

Ps 8:4-8 NKJV
What is man that You are mindful of him, and the son of man that You visit him? 5 For You have made him a little lower than the angels, And You have crowned him with glory and honor. 6 You have made him to have dominion over the works of Your hands; You have put all things under his feet, 7 All sheep and oxen — Even the beasts of the field, 8 The birds of the air, And the fish of the sea that pass through the paths of the seas.

Acts 10:11-16 NKJV
...and saw heaven opened and an object like a great sheet bound at the four corners, descending to him and let down to the earth. 12 In it were all kinds of four-footed animals of the earth, wild beasts, creeping things, and birds of the air. 13 And a voice came to him, "Rise, Peter; kill and eat." 14 But Peter said, "Not so, Lord! For I have never eaten anything common or unclean." 15 And a voice spoke to him again the second time, "What God has cleansed you must not call common." 16 This was done three times. And the object was taken up into heaven again.

=======

RELEASE CREATION TO PRAISE THE LORD
Bobby Conner tells of the time when the Lord sent him north specifically to the totem poles. When Bobby arrived, the Lord told him to bring them back to their original purpose which is to praise God.   Bobby saw the demonic creatures reigning over the carved poles, so he bound and cast the

devils out of them, and then loosed the poles back to their original purpose to praise the Lord.

We can also cast devils out of demonic carved rock images because even the rocks are meant to praise God.

Luke 19:40 NKJV
But He answered and said to them, "I tell you that if these should keep silent, the stones would immediately cry out ."

Rom 8:19-22 NKJV
For the earnest expectation of the creation eagerly waits for the revealing of the sons of God. 20 For the creation was subjected to futility, not willingly, but because of Him who subjected it in hope; 21 because the creation itself also will be delivered from the bondage of corruption into the glorious liberty of the children of God. 22 For we know that the whole creation groans and labors with birth pangs together until now.

Ps 69:34 NKJV
Let heaven and earth praise Him, the seas and everything that moves in them.

ANGELS AND WARFARE

In a prayer gathering, one of our intercessors received a vision that was most encouraging. I felt it was a revealing picture of what happens to our "warfare" prayers when we pray them. As a background to this vision, his daughter is in Spain going to school and we were praying from Oregon, USA.

She had called asking for prayer because she came in contact with a student that was involved with witchcraft, and she felt creepy and uncomfortable. They prayed over the phone, then later as an intercessory group we prayed again. We bound the powers of the enemy over her, broke off all

168

demonic assignments against her, and loosed the angels to send her deliverance. We also prayed a hedge of protection around her. After this, he received this wonderful vision:

His perspective was from the sky looking down upon the continents of the earth. Little lines extended out to all parts of the land masses. He understood these were the individual prayers of the people. They connected into three very large shafts of bright light coming from three continents and meeting together in the sky. These shafts of light appeared to carry substance, like living light moving upwards. At their point of intersection stood a bright angelic being, wielding a large sword.

The angel turned and pointed his sword to the region of Spain around Salamenca. A fierce white bolt of light came out of the sword and hit this region. When the angel had delivered the bolt, his sword came up and the living light ascending the shafts re-energized the sword for the next attack.

I was so blessed with he shared this vision! The scripture says, "Now faith is the substance of things hoped for, the evidence of things not seen." (Heb 11:1 KJV) Our faith is the living substance within those shafts of light and it releases all kinds of power in the spirit realm! What was even more encouraging was that we did not labor over our prayers for her, and there were only 8 of us in that room. If we only knew how powerful and important prayer is, we would never stop praying.

Bobby Conner saw a vision of some angels in heaven standing around bored. When He asked the Lord about them, He said that it was our responsibility to make sure they were sent. We have the authority in the name of Jesus to bind demonic powers and dispatch angels into any situation. I received two e-mails in response saying that we do not command angels, only God does that. I want to clear any misunderstandings. Nowhere in scripture does it say that we command angels, any more than we command God to do anything. There is a scripture that says angels heed the voice of His Word, but that does not mean they heed our voice or command. They listen for HIS WORD.

Ps 103:20 AMP
Bless (affectionately, gratefully praise) the Lord, you His angels, you mighty ones who do His commandments, hearkening to the voice of His word.

When I say we have the authority to bind demons and dispatch angels, I am speaking of the scripture, *"And I will give you the keys of the kingdom of heaven, and whatever you bind on earth will be bound in heaven, and whatever you loose on earth will be loosed in heaven."* (Matt 16:18-19 NKJV) When I pray, I bind the demonic powers and loose the angels to go forth on behalf of whatever situation needs attention.

It took the angel three weeks to fight through demonic resistance to get to Daniel. When he arrived, he said, *"Don't be frightened, Daniel, for your request has been heard in heaven and was answered the very first day you began to fast before the Lord and pray for understanding; that very day I was sent here to meet you. But for twenty-one days the mighty Evil Spirit who overrules the kingdom of Persia blocked my way. Then Michael, one of the top officers of the heavenly army, came to help me, so that I was able to break through these spirit rulers of Persia. Now I am here to tell you what will happen to your people, the Jews, at the end times-for the fulfillment of this prophecy is many years away."* (Dan 10:12-14 TLB)

What we do on earth works hand in hand with what is going on in heaven. The angels are working to fight through opposition and fasting is one of the tools to help them to fight through. Daniel fasted 3 weeks until he received his answer.

170

There are many tools in warfare, and Jesus gave us the keys of the kingdom to bind and loose. (Matt 16:18-19) In the Greek, the word "whatsoever" we bind or loose means "who, which or what." If we can bind a demon, we can loose their opposite, which is an angel.

I have been in many warfare situations at night where I see violent lightening clashes where binding the enemy and loosing the angels causes violent impacts against the darkness. As a weak vessel, it is very frightening and startling to experience these so close to the point of impact, but it makes me most grateful for the power to bind and loose. Things happen when we use the authority Jesus has given us!

WORD TO PONDER: INTERCESSORS STAND GUARD

I AM raising an army of intercessors who understand the significance of standing in the gap. They may be unseen by others, but they are not unseen by Me. These carry My authority into the spiritual realm and fight on behalf of others. They have been trained to stand strong against the enemy tide, and resist the forces sent against those they encircle. Together, they form a mighty wall of protection for the weaker vessels within.

Now is the time for those trained to defend and stand on behalf of those they love. Be strong, for the heavenly hosts fight with you. Be of great courage, for there are more with you than with the enemy. Stand in My favor and My grace. Know your own sins are forgiven and come into My courts with boldness, declaring defeat of the enemy's destructive forces, and victory for the overcomers who believe in My Name.

Arm yourselves with weapons of My authority. Keep your shields of faith high and quench the fiery darts with My

Word. Command the evil forces to retreat in the Mighty Name of Jesus. Loose the angels to go forth and fight. Use the battering rams of praise, worship and speaking My Name. Each blow causes a retreat. Be persistent and use your weapons over and over again, and the strongholds will fall. You will see victories all around you as you are willing to stand guard when I call you to do so. Be on the alert. I give you times of rest and times of war. Learn to discern them and you will learn to take advantage of both for My Kingdom's sake.

"And I sought for a man among them, that should make up the hedge, and stand in the gap before me for the land, that I should not destroy it:" (Ezekiel 22:30)

THE WALL, THE ANGELS AND REVIVAL

VISION 4/27/99:   Raising a Wall and Releasing the Angels

I was standing and searching the horizon a great distance away. I saw a wall burst forth and I barely had time to exclaim when its issuing was upon me: I saw an "invisible" wall raise up from the ground to the sky. Although not visible to the naked eye, I could see that it had substance as I saw millions of individual particles that were bursting with what looked like "living light."   I was looking at this wall from a side view, so I could not see the full front width of the wall, just its height from a narrow side angle bursting from earth upward. Now at the same time I saw the side view of the wall go upwards, I also saw this "living light" move towards me like what a wall of roaring water would do, filling the gaps and the spaces. To put it in other words, at a great distance way, I saw the starting place of this living wall and it rushed in two directions at the same time: perpendicular and horizontal.

172

Once I got over the shock of seeing this mass of living particles burst forth, I watched it form a barrier from earth to heaven and just stay there. It looked like it was an invisible shield of some sorts, but filled with this living light. I was standing at the end of the wall and could see and experience both sides of this wall.

On the right side of the wall I saw this airport runway filled with a large group of white hang glider planes with no motors. All were white hang gliders, but each were slightly different. Some were smaller, some larger, some had special shapes, but all made no noise. As though by command, like a huge flock of birds, I saw them swoop down the runway a few feet apart from one another. Now this was very intimidating because they were at one end of the runway, I was standing at the end of the runway, and they were coming towards me!

As I experienced this, I could actually feel my faith level. I watched them in mass coming toward me and I knew they were going to lift off and not run me over! As I watched many take off safely, I saw one smaller plane coming toward me and I began to doubt that it was going to make it without running me over! I felt like I was a "gonner." At the exact moment I lost my peace and began to doubt, that little plane lifted off the runway and started to wobble, wavering up and down in mid air. I saw that it was suspended between crashing and flying and **realized the connection between my faith and its ability to fly** so I stood firm that it was to rise and go forth. As I watched the plane respond to my standing firmly so that my faith did not wobble, I understood while still in the vision that these white hang glider planes were angels being sent forth.

On the other side of the wall of light, (to the left) I felt the compelling, almost gravitational pull of an evil force trying to drag me into a murky river to drown me. I fought it in Jesus Name and understood that in order to be safe from this evil

173

magnetic pull, I had to follow my conscience very carefully and this would keep me on the right side of the wall.

When I came out of the vision I understood the wall of living light represented the wall of protection built by those standing in the gap, and the angels were being loosed to go forth along side of this wall. The angels' abilities were directly related to our level of faith. The wall was a barrier of protection for the angels to go forth, separated from the demonic forces. Our faith level is directly tied to our life choices and whether we instinctively know if we are pleasing our Father in how we live moment to moment.

"And I sought for a man among them, that should make up the hedge, and <u>stand</u> (05975) in the gap before me for the land, that I should not destroy it: but I found none." (Eze 22:3)

The word "stand" [05975 `amad {aw-mad'}] in the Hebrew means: 1) to stand, remain, endure, take one's stand 1a) (Qal) 1a1) to stand, take one's stand, be in a standing attitude, stand forth, take a stand, present oneself, attend upon, be or become servant of 1a2) to stand still, stop (moving or doing), cease 1a3) to tarry, delay, remain, continue, abide, endure, persist, be steadfast 1a4) to make a stand, hold one's ground 1a5) to stand upright, remain standing, stand up, rise, be erect, be upright 1a6) to arise, appear, come on the scene, stand forth, appear, rise up or against 1a7) to stand with, take one's stand, be appointed, grow flat, grow insipid 1b) (Hiphil) 1b1) to station, set 1b2) to cause to stand firm, maintain 1b3) to cause to stand up, cause to set up, erect 1b4) to present (one) before (king) 1b5) to appoint, ordain, establish 1c) (Hophal) to be presented, be caused to stand, be stood before.

This standing is an active place of faith, whereby we endure and persist in the breach. For those who are involved in warfare, they know it is impossible to stand against a

174

demonic force if they are not heavily armed, especially with the favor of God. Always we war in the name of Jesus and under the covering of His blood, but there is also a place of favor that allows us to stand boldly. When we have displeased the Lord in some way during the day, we hear/see about it at night as the enemy is the first to put us on trial for such! **If we want to STAND in the gap, we have got to follow our conscience and please the Lord in our daily choices. Otherwise we DOUBT and this directly affects the angels** and also the erection of the wall beginning to circle around the world.

WORD TO PONDER: PRAY

If you truly understood what takes place the moment you pray, then you would truly never cease. When you pray, it sends the angels to go forth and make a way. Many operations take place behind the scenes to dove tail My Faithfulness into someone's life. One of the basic foundations of such is prayer. Angels are prepared and ready. They listen, awaiting to be dispatched with assignment. Prayer looses them to fight through obstacles, frees them to go forth, prepares events, and sets things in motion.

Did you know that when you pray for others, it has eternal value? Some day when you come here, you will stand before all those you have prayed for and will see how those simple requests made a difference in their lives. You will see entire destinies altered because you stopped to pray one simple prayer. Can you imagine it? If you only understood the power I have given into your hands to make a difference.

"Praying always with all prayer and supplication in the Spirit, and watching thereunto with all perseverance and supplication for all saints." (Ephesians 6:18)

175

PART FOUR: WARNINGS TO INTERCESSORS

SOUL POWER AND HEAD KNOWLEDGE

VISION 1/31/08: *I was moving toward the edge of some land and then I looked down and saw a lush peaceful green valley and a little town tucked in. I saw a little white church with a steeple.*

HEARD: *911 prayer meeting. Been so discouraged about how hard life is. When your emotions are involved. Prayer. Gusto. To help you get started. We the people. Never underestimate the power of influence. Soul power. Chain.*

HEARD: *Stranger things have happened. Head knowledge. The print out, it's wild all by itself. Do you want it? Yes I want it. It's beginning to make sense. Analyze and think it through. What did you come up with? Not much. Good girl, it's all by My Spirit.*

HEARD: *Dont be afraid. It's instinctual. I kept you. Wisdom. Training. Changes in My voice. It's all about love. Be kind and generous. Meek and lowly. Build one another up.*

HEARD: *Find common denominators and stick to them. Sticky. Watch. And find your place. Nothing could keep you from fitting in where you belong. It's instinctive. Movement. I am telling you. You got power. My Spirit. Fly and be free My dove.*

INSERT MILITARY MINDSET

EXCERPT RHEMA 1/21/08

HEARD: *If you can give me some backup I would sure appreciate it. What's wrong? Everything is not going as I planned. Military mindset.*

When I come, will there be faith? Condition. To choose. Abundance. To freely flow. In the right direction.

Rom 12:21 NKJV
Do not be overcome by evil , but overcome evil with good.

1 Peter 3:11 NKJV
Let him turn away from evil and do good; Let him seek peace and pursue it.

Rom 12:17-20 NKJV
Repay no one evil for evil . Have regard for good things in the sight of all men. 18 If it is possible, as much as depends on you, live peaceably with all men. 19 Beloved, do not avenge yourselves, but rather give place to wrath; for it is written, "Vengeance is Mine, I will repay," says the Lord.

WORD TO PONDER: PRAYER MEETINGS: OVERCOME SOUL POWER AND HEAD KNOWLEDGE 1/31/08

When you gather to pray there is wonderful synergy in loving unity, seeking My face, and the gathering together of men and angels. However resist using the human power of influence, which is soul power. Your influence is never in the strivings of flesh or voice, but in the power of My Spirit.

When you gather together in the round tables to hear what I AM saying, resist head knowledge when applying My Words. I have placed within you an instinctual discernment to resist the words of soul and flesh. I grant you wisdom when you ask for it. I bring My good gifts to your round tables as you seek My face for understanding. Learn to prophesy My good gifts out of the Spirit and not out of the soul and the demonic.

Learn to separate the profane demonic visions, and resist them. Do not empower them by prophesying them, or giving them credence. Stay simple concerning evil and do not dwell on it or linger there. Stand, resist the devil and he will flee. Close the doors to the distractions of war and gather together to seek My face and open the doors of heaven. Keep your focus on Me and not the devil. All demonic intent is distraction, and the enemy would derail My people and draw them into using the arm of flesh to fight endless battles.

Beloved ones, I want you to mount up in prayer and tongues so that you may fly and be free. I want you to soar above it all, and not be grounded in endless war. I AM the God of peace and My peace shall crush satan under your feet.

Rom 16:19-20 NKJV
I want you to be wise in what is good, and simple concerning evil. And the God of peace will crush Satan under your feet shortly. The grace of our Lord Jesus Christ be with you. Amen.

Zech 4:6-7 NKJV
Not by might nor by power, but by My Spirit,' Says the LORD of hosts. 'Who are you, O great mountain? Before Zerubbabel you shall become a plain! And he shall bring forth the capstone with shouts of "Grace, grace to it!

SOUL POWER VS THY KINGDOM COME

PIX 4/02/07: *I saw the # 153,* {arm force; shame}

OT:153 'edra` (Aramaic) (ed-raw'); an orthographical variation for OT:1872; an arm, i.e. (figuratively) power:
KJV - force.

NT:153
NT:153 aischunomai (ahee-skhoo'-nom-ahee); from aischos (disfigurement, i.e. disgrace); to feel shame (for oneself):
KJV - be ashamed.

178

CONFIRMATION CT: I opened my eyes and saw the clock time was 1:53.

COMMENT: I had a conversation yesterday about the power of force and using soul power upon a person to cause influence. It causes a lot of excess baggage.

HEARD: *May I have your attention please? We have got to get that off you.*

PIX: *I saw a man with a piece of luggage encasing his body.*

{In the same conversation I made the comment about carrying too much emotional soul baggage.}

CONFIRMATION: Someone emailed me today about how to pray for people without putting soul power / influence upon them. The following is my response.

HOW TO PRAY

I perceive you are concerned about Christian witchcraft and people declaring soul power and influence over others. I have a strong aversion to that, and I am always very careful about how I pray over people.

Mostly when I pray, it is when I hear something from the Lord, and then I pray into it. They are usually things where when I understand the season we are in, then I pray for the tools to get through it. They are things like courage, peace, understanding, guidance, revelation, help, protection, and the list goes on.

Like for instance recently I received a vision of a huge glistening white ocean liner. It was made of the identical material that I have seen before that was armor on God's army. I saw the ship had been at the dock and was now finally moving forward towards the bay. So prayers into that would be, letting go of the past and what is at the dock, the spiritual tools of direction to go, the provision while on board,

179

the weather, the water, everything needed to take the journey etc, etc.

If I hear something specific about a person as to what they are doing, I pray more specifically for the tools that I am inspired they need. If I know the person needs dominion taken, I bind the enemy and break off the assignments against that person then I counterbalance what has been broken off with the opposite spirit. For instance if the enemy plans death, then I bind and break it and loose abundant life. If he plans a lie, then I use my authority and then loose truth. This stops the opposition and looses the person to move into what they are needing to move forward in God. Sometimes when I take authority against the opposition, I pray scriptures against the enemy and on behalf of the person, declaring His Word to be released into their lives. If I have heard a rhema Word about the person sometimes I release that as a counterbalance against the demonic attempt.

Matt 6:6-13 NKJV
But you, when you pray, go into your room, and when you have shut your door, pray to your Father who is in the secret place; and your Father who sees in secret will reward you openly. And when you pray, do not use vain repetitions as the heathen do. For they think that they will be heard for their many words.

"Therefore do not be like them. For your Father knows the things you have need of before you ask Him. In this manner, therefore, pray:

Our Father in heaven, Hallowed be Your name. Your kingdom come., Your will be done on earth as it is in heaven. Give us this day our daily bread. And forgive us our debts, as we forgive our debtors. And do not lead us into temptation, but deliver us from the evil one. For Yours is the kingdom and the power and the glory forever. Amen.

HOW TO CLOSE THE DOORS TO BACKLASH

1. BUILD OUR METRON A STEP AT A TIME

The above examples of prayer, sacrifice and worship are ways to fight a safer battle without taking a direct "hit" from the enemy. These examples are important positions in the overall battle, yet are fought further away from the front lines. Using these weapons are different than actually addressing the enemy head-on.

The word "metron" comes from the scripture: "But we will not boast of things without our measure, but according to the measure (3358) of the rule (2583) which God hath distributed to us, a measure to reach even unto you." (2 Cor 10:13 KJV)

Metron is the Greek word metron (met'-ron) (3358) meaning a measure; by implication a limited portion (degree). Rule is the Greek word kanon (kan-ohn') (2583) from kane meaning: 1) A rod used to measure distance 2) A boundary or fixed space within the limits of which one's power of influence is confined as in (a) the province assigned to one (b) one's sphere of activity 3) metaphorically, any rule or standard, a principle or law of investigating, judging, living, acting. [From Thayer's Greek & Strongs]

The Lord has given us authority to bind the enemy and loose God's will. (Matt 16:19) He is wanting us to grow in our measure of authority against the enemy — first over the lack of freedom within our own lives, then our loved ones, then onto outside circumstances and territory that influence our lives - like work, school, church, etc. As we grow and overcome in the areas that touch our own lives then move onto bigger assignments, our circle of authority over the enemy grows and we are able to stand against greater odds. It is a step by step process of learning to obey the Lord and following Him in what He is asking us to overcome.

Problems arise when we step outside our metron. When the Jewish travelers were trying to cast out demons, one demon replied, "I know Jesus and I know Paul, but who are you?" (Acts 19:15 TLB) The demon injured them and they ran away naked. The demonic world knows us: our faith, our waverings, our strengths, our weaknesses. We must cover our own hedges first before we can expect to war safely on bigger issues.

The comforting part of learning to war in this manner is that He is sovereign and as long as we don't become presumptuous and take on more than He has assigned, then what He allows to touch our lives is strictly portioned one step at a time. (Ps 139) Everything must be cleared by Him first. We are the last day overcomers, and we will place the enemy under our feet and we will be victorious. But that only happens with Him divinely positioning us, and giving us our individual portions to complete. We will each have different assignments, but together we are taking territory.

2. RESIST SIN
The Lord said that we can not stand against our enemies until we remove the sin from our camp. (Josh 7:12) Disobedience to His Word is an open door for demons to set up camp in our lives. We are living in the day when the accuser has become very powerful because the hedge over our lives, cities, and countries has fallen through sin. God doesn't want the accuser having a foothold, but it leaves little choice when we are the ones giving the accuser ammunition. It all boils down to knowing and following God's Word. (Ps 119:11)

3. AVOID PRESUMPTION
Spiritual warfare is a serious business because we can not see with our natural eyes what is taking place. Therefore we are blind sided by unknown enemies, wondering what hit us! Our only hope is to learn to wait upon the Lord, Who does see, and only move forward in battle as He says to move.

This means we do not make plans for our lives, our families, our ministries, our churches, our neighborhoods, our towns, our countries, without first praying and asking God for His plan. If God is not behind the plan, we have no hope of ever standing against the obstacles that will come our way. It is hopeless before it ever gets started. The best remedy against presumption is to give God time. Revelation of His plan takes time as well as waiting for confirmation. (2 Cor 13:1) Waiting may be hard, but it is a lot easier than suffering great loss.

4. CLEANSE THE HOME
Sometimes cleansing the home is necessary. Countries with other religions actually send curses and spirits attached to the objects they export. There are millions of idols today, including children's toys. Many companies are turning to spiritual forces to manipulate the public. When searching your home and heart remember Romans 14 about eating meat sacrificed to idols. Pray and even anoint with oil things in your home, rebuke enemy attachments and loose blessings. Also remember 1 Thess 5:22 that says, "Abstain from all appearance of evil." If the item actually represents evil, why live with it? (Josh 7:12)

5. OVERCOME JUDGMENT WITH MERCY
Twenty eight years ago I learned a powerful lesson about opening the door for judgment to come upon my own life. I had become offended by the behavior and motives of a youth leader and started praying for him. The more I prayed, the more upset I became, and I finally talked to him, saying I had a Word from the Lord for him. Right after I delivered this "Word" the Lord showed me that I had pointed one finger, but had 3 fingers pointing back to myself. I suddenly realized I was guilty of the same motives and I repented. The deeper lesson I learned that day was that when we pray for our leaders we must cleanse our own hearts first. If we stay humble and pray for mercy, this will close doors of judgments to hit our own lives. If we judge, we will be

judged. This is a biblical promise. (Luke 6:37) The sooner we truly believe this, the sooner we will stop judging.

6. STAY IN UNITY
The demonic forces are gathering and uniting for greater impact. This is not a time to be an isolated believer, rather it is a time to unite, for we will all be much safer when united. There is greater authority in group prayer, and there is also a greater canopy of protection. The Lord is starting to unite His army, even joining leaders and ministries together for a synergistic effect. He said that 5 can chase 100 and 100 can chase 10,000. (Lev 26:8) That is the power of gathering in His Name.

7. KEEP OUR FOCUS
The enemy wants to challenge us into fighting a war on his terms. When this happens, our focus changes and we get our eyes onto the enemy instead of the Lord. I would like to share a story of some experiences because I believe it demonstrates the importance of what it means to keep our focus on the Lord.

Our city had a small riot that erupted from 200 anarchists demonstrating against capitalism. At the time the riot began, I came down with a very deep heavy burden pressing against my heart and stomach. I prayed, I warred, I spoke in tongues, I worshipped and it still lasted for about 5 hours before I found relief. Since I am fasting TV, I didn't know about the riot until the next day. Anarchists said their demonstration "got out of hand" causing $18,000 damage to local businesses, also busting driver's windows, and terrorizing motorists. (I wondered what "got out of hand" meant when they came prepared with metal bars, chains, rocks twice the size of softballs, and hoods to cover their faces?) Next they announced they were going to do their "demonstrations" the 3rd Friday of each month. It was easy to figure out where my burden came from especially when it lasted the same duration of the 5 hour demonstration.

I had received a dream in October 98 when I understood that the enemy's desire was to bring the spirits of lawlessness and riots to the streets, so that it would drive the righteous out of the cities. I felt sick. I had just witnessed a beginning seed of this lawless spirit and knew exactly what the enemy wanted to birth. I kept thinking, 200 people inspired by anarchy can eventually cause the righteous to move away? Yes, when empowered by some heavy-duty principalities.

After the understanding came, I started asking the Lord to raise up the local churches to pray against this. I said, "Lord, it isn't right that we can just let the enemy walk in and take over!" Within days of the riot, our little church happened to have a training conference on demonic warfare and deliverance. Unbeknownst to us, evidently Goliath listened and came knocking on our door that night.

That night the Lord told me the enemy was wanting to break through the hedge and He wanted me to stand. (Eph 6:13) I had no idea what He meant, but I found out. Around midnight a demonic presence appeared in one of our intercessor's bedroom. They got up, took authority and anointed their place with oil. One hour later the same presence jumped on the foot of another intercessor while she was sleeping. The next hour I saw a hole open in the spirit realm and I felt an overwhelming evil presence. I woke up screaming. (I have had many warfare experiences in 15 years and only woke up screaming one other time.) In spite of it, I stood against it and went back to sleep! The next night, I not only felt it, but heard it. It was a union of 6 powerful forces that had joined together and had come to challenge. Two of the names were intimidation and rebellion. I stood against them for hours, and awoke feeling like I had gotten nowhere.

That morning I awoke to a TP'd and fouled yard. My husband and I anointed our property, and everything we could think of with oil, praying and commanding the enemy to stay off our turf. That night my husband and I both saw them. I also felt and heard them, literally wrestling in hand to hand combat for 2½ hours. During all of these experiences, I continued to plead the blood of Jesus Christ, bound them, and commanded them to leave in Jesus Name. The next night, the minute I closed my eyes I heard and felt the same presence. It felt significantly weaker by about 70%, but I had HAD IT. "THAT'S IT! I'M CALLING IN THE TROOPS!" I called Anna (there is nothing like a mother bear's prayers for her cub) and told her some of this, and she began to war over the phone. As she was commanding, I heard the Lord say, "Warrior." I felt very comforted and had enough peace to go back to sleep.

I slept some, then finally I heard the Lord! "She belongs to ME says the Lord. MY bride!" When I heard this, the emphasis was on ME and MY. I had instant peace! I felt like a love-sick bride whose chivalrous Husband stepped in to rescue her. I felt so deeply loved after such intimidating experiences. I turned over with a smile and slept blissfully the rest of the night. The next morning I called Anna and she was joyfully laughing. She had heard the Lord say, "I perceive guard duty is a bit too heavy!" The first words out of my mouth were, "DUH!!!!" That made her laugh, because that is exactly what she had said too!

"For we do not wrestle against flesh and blood, but against principalities, against powers, against the rulers of the darkness of this age, against spiritual hosts of wickedness in the heavenly places. Therefore take up the whole armor of God, that you may be able to withstand in the evil day, and having done all, to stand." (Eph 6:12-13 NKJ)

There was a lesson in this. During this four day "adventure" I kept searching my heart and asking the Lord for understanding. I searched my heart to make sure that I personally had not challenged this "challenger" when the riot came. I don't remember doing so, rather I prayed that the Lord would raise up intercessors and prayer in the churches. Lord, have I unknowingly sinned? Have I been presumptuous? Have I gone outside my metron? I could not come up with any reason why suddenly this blast would come to our door and want to force its way in. **Finally I understood**.

One of our intercessors shared a vision she'd had years ago when she had been in heavy warfare, and was taken up to the Lord. She kept looking behind her and the enemy was standing right behind her. The Lord took her face several times and turned her eyes back on Him. As she did, she got closer and closer to the Lord. Some time passed and then He told her to look back. The enemy was very small and in the distance. She got the point. We are called to keep our eyes, our focus on Him. We are to pursue Him.

Because we pursue the Lord, we naturally suffer resistance from the enemy. However, it is a result of going after the Lord, not after the enemy. Without giving the details of our warfare conference, I could see so clearly that our focus changed for a brief moment and opened Goliath's door. Warfare should always be a result of our pursuit of the Lord and keeping our focus upon Him. If you are suffering backlash and have covered every breach in your wall you can think of, perhaps all that is needed is to get your eyes back onto the Lord. I am reminded of Smith Wigglesworth' life when he saw satan appear at his bedside. Smith said, "Oh, it's only you," and turned over and went back to sleep.
May we learn to use our weapons of prayer, sacrifice, worship, and authority safely. May we learn to cover the breaches in our own lives so that we can stand for our cities without retaliation, in Jesus Name.

FOLLOW YOUR CONSCIENCE: DIVINE RESTRAINTS

DREAM: I was given a dream in direct answer to what I prayed before going to sleep. I had asked the Lord to teach me what we can do as human beings to help the angels fight on our behalf.

I was searching and investigating treasures of natural rock formations. The ones I had were beautiful. As I was looking I saw six or so angels floating above my head. It was funny that I didn't realize they were angels even though they were floating. But when I saw them join their ethereal hands together, I realized, "Oh they must be angels!" Then I noticed they were floating above me where ever I went.

In the distance I saw mountains and rugged terrain. Thinking it might be a good place to look for rocks, I looked at the angels, and said to one with intent in my action, "Bye!" Then walking in the direction I wanted to go, I saw a white line painted on the ground about 5" wide, and wondered why it was there.

I crossed over the line and heard in the distance some enemies whose job it was to trap people who had gone over the line. I looked back and saw that the angels had not followed me but were still on the other side of the line. I suddenly realized I was in danger. I turned around, and immediately instead of the easy way I had arrived, the terrain had changed and was straight up. With great urgency, I had to use both hands, fingers, feet and legs to pull myself straight up a rock cliff. It was extremely difficult and I felt the gravity of not only my weight, but earth's gravity against me. I could hear the enemy getting closer and I knew I was in danger.

I saw the angels on the other side of the line and cried for help. Only one came, and that was the one to whom I had said "good-bye.". He grabbed a hold of the back of my shirt and held on. But I still had to climb. It was so difficult, I said to myself, "Why doesn't he just fly me up there, I know he can fly and it would be simple!" I was perturbed that I had to work so hard. As I was climbing, I felt that this angel had put himself in danger to come to me, just as I had put myself in danger. The reason being, he and I were outnumbered on this side of the white line.

Finally we were on the other side of the line and I was walking straight and easy again. I looked back and saw a man whose feet were just on the good side of the line. He had a pack on his back and the pack extended over the line to the other side. I looked up and there was an evil spirit towering over him. The spirit's feet were restrained on the other side of the line. Because the man's pack was still on the bad side of the line, the spirit grabbed the pack, and thus the man. I was wishing I could have helped him but knew I couldn't as it had something to do with free will.

Possible Interpretation: I believe this dream means the enemy is placed behind divine restraints and not able to hold us captive if we are in God's approved location. In this dream there are three issues enabling the enemy to snare us. The most important and obvious issue is not to cross the line of our conscience, leaving behind God's approval. The second is to not flirt with danger. Making choices that are not necessarily sin, but definitely not edifying is getting too close for comfort. The third is not to carry excess baggage. The man was being obedient by being on the right side of the line, but what he was carrying inside his pack was not. He was attached to something that went against his conscience, and this enabled the evil being to grab the attachment, and thus the man. The lesson here is to let go of the sins that easily beset us and leave them a good distance behind. We can not keep sin in our back pack and expect to stay out of harm's way.

When I walked away from God's approval, I placed myself behind enemy lines by my own volition. Once I realized my mistake and cried for help, I was perturbed that I had to work so hard to get back to that safe place. Based upon other rhema I have had, I can see several reasons for having to work so hard.

One; Remember the point of the previous dream where there was a stalemate of equal forces battling over the poor pathetic man's freedom - it took his vote to tip the scales of justice.

Two; Sometimes it takes major warfare to get someone free, and that doesn't happen without the backup of extra warring angels.

Three; In past intercession experiences where warfare was involved, the Lord told me there were delays because of stalemates, as there was not enough prayer support. We may wonder why, when there is a two thirds versus one third principle of angelic forces in the heavens. Our two thirds are not all warriors and they each have different assignments, gifts and skills. Neither do all warriors fight the same battles. In application, without the backup of our own prayers of authority, outside prayer support, and angelic forces, it is very difficult to climb up and out behind enemy lines.

In this dream the angel was guarding my back but I still had to climb out. It's very possible that part of the reason I had to climb and work so hard was so I would remember the importance of the white line next time around! The whole thing could have been avoided if I had followed my conscience in the first place.

PART FIVE:
EXAMPLES OF INTERCESSIONS

BOB JONES IMPORTANCE OF PRAYER

When Bob Jone's died and went to heaven on 8/8/75, when he came back, he depended upon the intercessors to pray him back to health. The following is a quote from a transcript off a tape.

"The Lord said, "I want you to go back and touch the church and speak to the church of what I am going to do in these last days." So I told Him I would come back. I came back. I thought that when I come back into my body I would be healed. As I came back I saw 2 of the biggest angels I have ever seen. I know who they are. They are the resurrection angels. And I saw the death spirit and he left when I came back in. And when I went back into the body I wasn't healed. The pain was there and I couldn't understand why. And I was gone probably for about 3 hours. The pain was there and I said, "What's going on Lord?" And then I heard a phone ring. And I saw people answering the phone and they were saying, "Bob Jones needs prayer." And they would start praying and I felt better. And it was a Friday.

People kept praying and it kept increasing and increasing. And then people came over and prayed for me Friday night til the pain wasn't hardly there. And then Friday night, Sat morning at 3 o clock the last person quit praying for me. I could see who was praying for me. The pain was coming back and I thought, "Boy it's going to be a long time." And then I saw an old sister who wasn't thought highly of in the church because she didn't take too many baths. She always sat in the last seat in back. And she cleaned offices for a living. She got up early in the morning and cleaned offices. And her phone rang and she answered it. She got up at 3 o clock in the morning and started praying for me and I went to sleep. And then she had to go to work at 5 and others began to pray for me, so Saturday was pretty good. It went pretty well. People came over Saturday and I thought, "Well I know He sent me back down here to live." And prayer and intercession sure made the difference.

And Saturday night it went on pretty good until about 3 o clock and all the other prayer ended. Except hers. She got up and went to praying for me again. She prayed for me until about 7 o clock. She didnt have to work on a Sunday. At 7 o clock was the worst time that I saw because there was no prayer. People were going to church.

And it was really bad until about 10:05. At 10 o'clock, Viola asked me how are you doing? I told her I was worse then than I had ever been and I was swelling so bad I couldn't even get out of bed. At 10:05 I became totally normal, totally delivered. I got up and we went to church and I testified of it.

I found out the value of prayer. And I found out the value of not having an opinion about saints. I found out the value of ministry. That one saint was able to void all of it to where I could sleep."

PRAYER MEETING: FREE THE DESPERATE

Tonight during prayer I had the burden for those who could not pray for themselves and I shed tears over them in prayer.

PIX 7/14/07: *I saw a hand using a fan to fan some coals. The coals were called Desperation.*

PIX: I saw a lightning rod come down at the same time our right hand was reaching up and the power of God came upon the hand.

Luke 11:20 NKJV
But if I cast out demons with the finger of God , surely the kingdom of God has come upon you.

CONFIRMATION; Pastor called for those who needed deliverance from addictions to come forward tonight for prayer. As I pondered this I realized that sometimes God allows us to become desperate in our need so we will finally get help.

WORD O' GRAM: FREEDOM

Fully liberated.

Renounced bondage.

Everlasting joy.

Eternal blessings.

Domination broken.

Overcoming abundant life.

More than enough.

Gal 5:1 NKJV
Stand fast therefore in the liberty by which Christ has made us free, and do not be entangled again with a yoke of bondage.

Gal 5:13 NKJV
For you, brethren, have been called to liberty; only do not use liberty as an opportunity for the flesh, but through love serve one another.

2 Cor 3:17 NKJV
Now the Lord is the Spirit; and where the Spirit of the Lord is, there is liberty.

PRAYER MEETING: UNITY AND THE BREAKER ANOINTING

BRIEF IMPRESSION 5/12/07: Tonight in pre-prayer I heard the intercessor next to me say the word "angels" when she was speaking in tongues. I leaned over and told her that, so I prayed that the angels would come and that tonight we would experience an Explosion in the Spirit. I had the impression of something so powerful happening that the

Lord would send forth a lightning rod down from heaven and scatter our enemies. I did not see this, but asked for it as it was impressed upon my heart.

TENACITY: We ended up having massive unified warfare. It was one of the most powerful prayer meetings I have ever been in. Each level seemed to grow after the next. We would think we were done, then someone would say, we are not yet done, we need to continue to press through! We had never had such pressing through, where we would become quieter and then another call and wave of His Spirit to press on. After several had lead out in prayer with the rest loudly backing in tongues, we had ended up all facing the same direction and clapping our hands together slowly in one united sound. It reverberated in the room and I knew this was the sound of God's army marching – the sound of feet in perfect cadence upon the earth. We had united with heaven's army and it was a powerful moment.

At the very end of this, I opened my mouth to release one long, loud sound for as long as I could release it in one breath. Then I took another deep breath and did the same sound again. I felt led to do this over and over again as though relentlessly. This repeated over and over again. Soon the whole room was doing the same thing, first I would sound and then they responded in the same. Pastor ran into the other room and brought back his shofar and blew it and we responded to that. I suddenly realized that the sound that we were making together was a cross between a warrior's cry and an announcement from a clarion trumpet.

OPENED EARS: Then I heard a loud angel say, "The breaker anointing." The voice was heavily impacting and not the Lord's still small voice. As soon as I heard him, I was hit by the power of God, I doubled over into the birthing position and yelled out several times with trembling. It was a brief moment of travail.

INTERPRETATION OF TONGUES: Right after that I had an interpretation of one of the words the intercessor spoke in tongues. She clearly said, "Crescendo!"

(That is a musician's term from a building up or climax. No kidding, I smiled at that!!!)

QUIET TIME: During our time of waiting upon the Lord after this, I heard the Lord's still small voice.

HEARD; *Tenacity. I show Myself strong on behalf of those who unite. Follow through. Dominion. Shatter their ranks. Explosive union by My hand.*

CONFIRMATION: During share time one of the intercessors said she heard, The army of the Lord brings break through.

CHURCH: Worship was powerful tonight at church. Pastor's wife stood up and proclaimed the following scripture. I felt it was a confirmation that what I had sensed at the beginning of prayer meeting, that we would have an explosion and it would result from the lightning of God. God indeed scattered our enemies.

2 Sam 22:14-16 NKJV
"The LORD thundered from heaven, And the Most High uttered His voice. He sent out arrows and scattered them; Lightning bolts, and He vanquished them. Then the channels of the sea were seen, The foundations of the world were uncovered, At the rebuke of the LORD, at the blast of the breath of His nostrils.

THE WORD FROM THE BREAKER ANGEL: Breaking Through Barrenness

When I got home from church I had the following email sent to me and knew it was a confirmation to one of the intercessions that had taken place during pre-prayer. It was something that was warred for and then released to us. It was a direct confirmation to what I had experienced at pre-prayer, what I had sent in an email just prior to leaving for church, and the picture I saw during church.

EMAIL CONFIRMATION: "Two days ago I had a new experience with the Lord and I have been praying and thinking about it. I was first worshiping Him with songs as the Spirit gave them to me. I started to hear a sound, a note that came closer and closer to me, entered me and then through me the natural realm as I started to sing that one note only.

When I asked the Lord what was happening I felt Him say that note, that heavenly sound was a weapon against a particular spirit in the area: the spirit of barrenness.

So I just kept singing that note. I felt that one note had a form, a depth, a substance and I have never heard such a thing before. It was nothing of me, totally separate, just coming through me as if through a funnel. I also sensed that it literally annoyed demonic spirits and they were expressing their dislike clearly."

CONFIRMATION: Just prior to going to church I sent a long email to someone about releasing the seeds that God has planted inside of us. The very end of the email was what I had heard on 10/21/04:

HEARD: *Harvest. I planted you. Right on. Don't let go. Promises.*

PIX: *I was standing on a bridge looking down upon a river that was flowing with a gentle current.*

HEARD: *When we were at lunch you could hear the Savior say to believe. All these Words so lovingly planted. Trust Me. The power of My seed. Is not barren. There is beyond the heart that is depairin'. So trust Me as we win this war over dead faith.*

The trust that You planted is given freely. A harvest of seed is coming your way. A harvest of seeds bearing after its kind. Woa.

VISION DURING CHURCH: I saw a little acorn and knew it was destined to be a huge oak tree. I felt the acorn was either dead, dormant or barren faith. And so I cupped my hands around it and began to blow upon it. I blew 4 times. And each time was a long blast of hot air. My hands became very hot and I knew this seemingly dead acorn came to life. I had a rush of heat all over me. And then I held it in my hand, open palm, and sprinkled salt upon it to represent His irrevocable covenant, and then I dug a hole, planted it, and poured rain down upon it.... I pantomimed all of this with my eyes closed.

I am sure if anyone was looking they must have thought it very strange. Smile! Let's just face it, intercessors are radical believers and what they do best is birth on earth what God speaks in heaven.

VISION: Then I was very gratified to see a picture of a green spout come through the broken shell and I knew it had come to life and would bear fruit after its kind and come into its full destiny.

CONFIRMATION: Pastor preached out of Isa 61: 1-7 and I noticed one of the verses in there was the following:

Isa 61:3 AMP
To grant [consolation and joy] to those who mourn in Zion — to give them an ornament (a garland or diadem) of beauty instead of ashes, the oil of joy instead of mourning, the garment [expressive] of praise instead of a heavy, burdened, and failing spirit — that they may be called oaks of righteousness [lofty, strong, and magnificent, distinguished for uprightness, justice, and right standing with God], the planting of the Lord, that He may be glorified.

FINAL NOTE: I just finished typing this from last night's meeting where one of the things broken through was barrenness. Today is Mother's day, 2007.

One of the things we do in our family is celebrate the day our son was conceived. This year I said this to him: "When you came to us, you were a little tiny dot inside us, and God put both together and here you are, a MIRACLE. Always remember that every miracle begins as little tiny dots full of God potential."

PRAYER MEETING: BREAK THE DEMONIC STRONGHOLDS OF THE MIND

HEARD 4/17/07: Tonight at church I heard the words, *"distraction and divided mind."*

CONFIRMATION: Then later one of our intercessors declared this scripture:

2 Cor 10:5 NKJV
... bringing every thought into captivity to the obedience of Christ...

TONGUES BREAKTHROUGH THE MYRIAD OF THOUGHTS:

Later there was a rising up of warrior tongues coming from the end of the room. I felt a rush of the Spirit of God sweep through the room from their burst of tongues and then I saw all these tiny scissors in rapid and blurring cutting motions. It was impressed upon me that there was a lattice work of threads, ropes and vines and the scissors were located in the holes of the lattice and they were rapidly cutting through these invisible cords.

I felt that each of these scissors were the instruments of our individual ministering angels and they were uniting to cut the myriad of distractions and divided minds. My heart was filled with faith and I felt this could even extend to those who were under the influence of ADD, the deaf and dumb spirit, and all forms of memory loss.

CONFIRMATION: Later when we were still before the Lord and went around the room to share, pastor said that the Word he had received was to "CUT IT!!" It was a command from the Lord.

ANOTHER INTERCESSOR quoted the following scripture during share time.

Rom 12:2 NKJV
I beseech you therefore, brethren, by the mercies of God, that you present your bodies a living sacrifice, holy, acceptable to God, which is your reasonable service. And do not be conformed to this world, but be transformed by the renewing of your mind, that you may prove what is that good and acceptable and perfect will of God.

CONFIRMATION: That was confirmed to me, because another word I heard His voice say during our prayers was the phrase, "It's a reasonable sacrifice." In this context of our thinking, I feel the Lord is saying to present our minds to Him, which is a logical, rational choice over our thinking.

1 Cor 2:14-16 NKJV
But the natural man does not receive the things of the Spirit of God, for they are foolishness to him; nor can he know them, because they are spiritually discerned. But he who is spiritual judges all things, yet he himself is rightly judged by no one. For "who has known the mind of the LORD that he may instruct Him?" But we have the mind of Christ.

PRAYER: Lord we yield to Your call upon our thought life, our brains, our minds. We confess and repent of our negative thinking that does not line up with Your Word and Your heart for us. We repent of dwelling on the things of the world and not disciplining our own selves to turn away and turn off thoughts that grieve You.

We bind the demonic spirits of distraction and divided mind and command them to be broken off us in the Name of Jesus. We lay hands upon our minds and command all demonic strongholds to be removed. We declare the blood of Jesus to flow in and through our brains that they will be redeemed and renewed according to the Word of God.

We ask that You grant us the mind of Christ and restore to us that which has been stolen. We ask that You will transform us by the renewing of our minds. in the Name of Jesus we ask. Amen.

Eph 4:23-24 NKJV
...and be renewed in the spirit of your mind, and that you put on the new man which was created according to God, in true righteousness and holiness.

UNITED INTERCESSORS: AN ARROW IN THE SKY

Consider the geese when they fly in the sky,
Lined up like an arrow, when they pass by.
In oneness they move, united in synch.
One after the other, they are so linked.

They move forward to comfortable weather.
It is their instinct to stay together
As I plant in their hearts this common ground,
Of moving on and following the sound.

They are noisy as they move overhead.
While some stay for winter, these press on instead.
With vision and purpose they flap their wings.
Through the cold air, forsaking winter's sting.

Taking the brunt of the opposing air
The lead bird is strengthened against what's there.
I pour into him the strength of My might

As he seeks the landscape for promise in sight.

As he takes his place all others follow suit,
Then together they move on in one pursuit.
He takes his watch at the tip of the arrow.
Setting forehead like flint through bone and marrow.

He's fulfilling his time with faithful passing.
He can hear other flocks gathered and massing.
It strengthens resolve to proceed past winter,
Behind him is frozen from cold endured. .

Before him is comfort and warmth and rest.
As he flaps his wings opposing the test.
He knows My way through instinct in his heart.
With resolve inside, he shield's fiery darts.

From the unit he's leading, he takes the brunt.
Their sound from behind braces him out front.
Should he grow tired, they all change places.
For another to watch, releasing My graces.

So consider the birds as they fly in the air,
And know your position to stay in prayer.
I AM moving you forward to a better place.
Follow My calling and soar with My pace.

INTERCESSION FOR THE DAVIDS AND MICHALS

11/12/06: A spirit of weeping came over me at church tonight. I felt the deep pain of those marriages who are unequally yoked where the men have loved the Presence and anointing of God and they have been called fools and were despised by way of demonic forces through their loved ones. I wept deep, deep sobs over their pain, as they have sacrificed so deeply in yearnings for their brides to follow them in ushering in the ark of God's Presence. At one point I saw a man in a bridal white tux carrying his bride in his arms with so much labor because he did not want to leave her behind.

Earlier during worship, I heard the demonic continue to say, "fool!" and I saw a huge rock in the path. I understood the rock was the stone of offense where those who were willing to be fools for Jesus had become rocks to stumble the religious people and who were branded as fools. It was not until I felt David's heart for his bride, who had looked down upon him and despised the purity of his abandoned worship, did I understand that he was a type of the fool for Jesus. He had chosen to be nakedly transparent in his testimony of his love and pursuit of the Lord and suffered deeply for it.

I saw how many men had moved forward in God a few paces, then once again offered liberal sacrifices. I understood that many men have walked out an intercession with the heart of Jesus over His beloved Bride, to carry her, stir her, wake her, draw her out of religion, and into intimacy with Him to become equally yoked with Him. They were doing so at great, great cost.

I asked forgiveness for all those despisers who dethroned the Word of God. I asked forgiveness for all those who dared to call common that which was holy. I asked for mercy over those who had despised those who wholeheartedly responded to God's Presence. I sobbed and wept and prayed. I knew the Holy Spirit had become grieved. I begged the Lord for the unequally yoked marriages, that He would give the Michals a second chance. That He would deliver them from despising the Holy Spirit and give them altercations just like He did Saul on the road to Damascus. I felt no answer to this prayer as though it was closed and this made me cry more.

Then the Spirit of prophesy came upon me and I saw that David was covered with fool's gold. As the ark of His Presence was ushered into the city, the gold from the ark began to replace the fool's gold and cover David with the pure gold. And when David became pure gold like the ark, he had the heart of God's mercy seat within him. I saw that all David chose to touch would turn to gold and it was given to David the choice to touch anyone he chose with God's golden Presence, including his wife with golden mercy. If she received, she would receive through her husband at his hand. It was his right to give or withhold and I saw the power of intercession as it truly was - over those whose hands and mouths are not innocent.

REVELATION: Later as I thought about the intercession, I remembered that Michal was the daughter of Saul. There has been a long war between the house of Saul and the house of David. Throughout the years, the Holy Spirit has become very grieved with those who took His anointing and placed it under their own control and for their own gain. Thus His fresh anointing and outpouring has turned to the house of David. It is in the anointing of David, that He will bring in the blessing of His Presence and bring mercy to all who repent from the house of Saul.

2 Sam 6:13-16 NKJV
And so it was, when those bearing the ark of the LORD had gone six paces, that he sacrificed oxen and fatted sheep. Then David danced before the LORD with all his might; and David was wearing a linen ephod. So David and all the house of Israel brought up the ark of the LORD with shouting and with the sound of the trumpet. Now as the ark of the LORD came into the City of David, Michal, Saul's daughter, looked through a window and saw King David leaping and whirling before the LORD; and she despised him in her heart.

Job 22:25-30 NKJV
Yes, the Almighty will be your gold and your precious silver; For then you will have your delight in the Almighty, and lift up your face to God. You will make your prayer to Him, He will hear you, and you will pay your vows. You will also declare a thing, and it will be established for you; So light will shine on your ways. When they cast you down, and you say, 'Exaltation will come!' Then He will save the humble person.

He will even deliver one who is not innocent; Yes, he will be delivered by the purity of your hands."

PRAYER & SUPERNATURAL DELIVERANCE

We heard of a miracle that happened this week with someone we know, and prayer was directly related to saving his life. A fellow was on his way to school to drive and his car went off the edge of the road and landed upside down in the bottom of the river, 20 feet submerged. Everything was dark and he knew he was going to die so he prayed that the Lord would take him to heaven. Then he suddenly had the thought to open his eyes and take a peek. He saw light and thought perhaps he should at least try to get out! So he unbuckled his seat belt and realized the car window had broken out, so he swam through the window, and followed the light UP. He swam to shore, climbed back up the bank and his Dad was a few minutes behind him driving to work and picked him up! They did 7 hours of tests on him, put a shunt in his ear to drain, sewed up his cuts and sent him home. He is totally fine, and drove to school a couple days later.

Prior to this, his Mom woke up in the middle of the night with a burden to pray for him. Not only that but another friend woke that same morning with a vision of someone all bloody and wet and so she prayed.

INTERCESSION OVER GRIEVING THE HOLY SPIRIT

HEARD 1/27/08: *We should tell her. Comfort her. Let her see.*

HEARD: *Pain medicine. My daughter.*

PIX: *I saw a mother holding a baby. She shrunk down to the floor, fitting into a very tiny space as though they were both sitting in a round baby walker. It was the only space left for them to occupy.*

HEARD: *How much room do we have? Will you align with truth?*

Mark 14:33-42 NKJV
He began to be troubled and deeply distressed. 34 Then He said to them, "My soul is exceedingly sorrowful, even to death. Stay here and watch ." 35 He went a little farther, and fell on the ground, and prayed that if it were possible, the hour might pass from Him. 36 And He said, "Abba, Father, all things are possible for You. Take this cup away from Me; nevertheless, not what I will, but what You will." 37 Then He came and found them sleeping, and said to Peter, "Simon, are you sleeping? Could you not watch one hour? 38 Watch and pray, lest you enter into temptation. The spirit indeed is willing, but the flesh is weak." 39 Again He went away and prayed, and spoke the same words. 40 And when He returned, He found them asleep again, for their eyes were heavy; and they did not know what to answer Him. 41 Then He came the third time and said to them, "Are you still sleeping and resting? It is enough! The hour has come; behold, the Son of Man is being betrayed into the hands of sinners.

REVELATORY EXPERIENCE AND INTERCESSION: Recently I have been experiencing a very heavy grieving of the Holy Spirit. Although I have suffered this many times, I had not experienced this level of the Holy Spirit's grieving since the early 80's. I would feel perfectly fine and then suddenly something very deep would rise up in my spirit like a wave of overwhelming grief. I had to be sure this was not a demonic spirit of grief or even perhaps my own broken soul that the Lord was drawing out. I had been taking authority, praying and doing everything I could to wash this grief out of me including asking for prayer in the prayer line. Tonight as I was praying over these experiences, the Lord took me into a very intimate experience of revelation and intercession.

I suddenly felt the Holy Spirit knocking on the doors of the hearts of mankind. With great longings and yearnings of unreciprocated love, He was saying, "Do you love Me? Do you want Me? How much room do you have in your life for Me? How much of Me do you accept?" With those longings of intent, He would knock on our heart until we opened up to sup with Him. And when we opened up to Him, it gave Him pleasure and comfort just to be with us and have us listen to Him and commune.

We had many doors in our heart-home and when He knocked, He might gain entrance to some, but in others we would keep our doors closed and not let Him in. He continued knocking on closed doors until we were "set" in our decisions and He had the answer to His quest. Then He withdrew from knocking and stayed within the confines of whatever boundary we allowed Him. I was overwhelmed with His love, and desire, and yearning to be allowed access into our lives. And then I saw the truth that He had also been knocking on the doors of our families, homes, churches, denominations, schools, cities, states, and countries. He has had this same quest throughout all history. He has wanted to find a resting place, where He could dwell in reciprocal love and be fully accepted and embraced.

I saw that we ourselves set our own boundaries for Him. And to the same degree that we have resisted His knock, we have raised up boundaries that have either kept Him at bay, resisted Him, grieved Him, quenched Him, despised His voice, scorned His Words, or defamed Him and spoken evil of Him. I felt the flooding of His heart; all He wanted was our reciprocal love.

As I understood this, that same grief rose up inside and I sobbed, and sobbed and sobbed. I have never gone through such an experience, because this pain was not my own pain. Tonight when I sobbed it was not for me, it was for HIM. I was so deeply impacted by the suffering of the Holy Spirit... the depth of His love, His longing, His longsuffering and relentlessness to keep knocking and trying to find someone who will listen and give Him room. I cried for Him and kept telling Him how deeply sorry I was for His pain and all that we had done to Him to resist Him. I asked the Father's forgiveness for all mankind for we have pushed Him away, and treated His heart and Word so glibly.

I could not even fathom the longsuffering He has gone through to have suffered the same quest through out all of history. His love is so deep, so passionate, so intense that no amount of rejection and suffering has kept Him from His quest! He has been relentless to find His resting place where His fullness can dwell without restraints, without measure, and with the fullest expression.

DEEPER REVELATION - TO EXTINGUISH THE HOLY SPIRIT

After I sobbed for Him, He brought the following scriptures into memory:

Luke 13:34-35 NKJV
"O Jerusalem, Jerusalem, the one who kills the prophets and stones those who are sent to her! How often I wanted to gather your children together, as a hen gathers her brood under her wings, but you were not willing! 35 See! Your house is left to you desolate; and assuredly, I say to you, you shall not see Me until the time comes when you say, 'Blessed is He who comes in the name of the LORD!'"

1 Thess 5:19-22 NKJV
Do not quench the Spirit. Do not despise prophecies. Test all things; hold fast what is good. Abstain from every form of evil.

1 Thess 5:20-22 AMP
Do not spurn the gifts and utterances of the prophets {do not depreciate prophetic revelations nor despise inspired

instruction or exhortation or warning}. But test and prove all things {until you can recognize} what is good; {to that} hold fast. Abstain from evil {shrink from it and keep aloof from it} in whatever form or whatever kind it may be.

Mark 3:28-30 NKJV
"Assuredly, I say to you, all sins will be forgiven the sons of men, and whatever blasphemies they may utter; but he who blasphemes {987} against the Holy Spirit never has forgiveness, but is subject to eternal condemnation" — 30 because they said, "He has an unclean spirit."

WORD STUDY
After I pondered those scriptures, I did a word study and saw something I had not seen before in this word study:

1 Thess 5:19-22 NKJV
Do not quench {4570} the Spirit. Do not despise {1848} prophecies. Test all things; hold fast what is good. Abstain from every form of evil.

QUENCH
sbennumi

NT:4570 sbennumi (sben'-noo-mee); a prolonged form of an apparently primary verb; to extinguish (literally or figuratively):
KJV - go out, quench.

DESPISE
exoutheneo
NT:1848 exoutheneo (ex-oo-then-eh'-o); a variation of NT:1847 and meaning the same:
KJV - contemptible, despise, least esteemed, set at nought.

NT:1847
NT:1847 exoudenoo (ex-oo-den-o'-o); from NT:1537 and a derivative of the neuter of NT:3762; to make utterly nothing of, i.e. despise:
KJV - set at nought. See also NT:1848.

BLASPHEMY
NT:987
NT:987 blasphemeo (blas-fay-meh'-o); from NT:989; to vilify; specially, to speak impiously:
KJV - (speak) blaspheme (-er, -mously, -my), defame, rail on, revile, speak evil.

NT:989
NT:989 blasphemos (blas'-fay-mos); from a derivative of NT:984 and NT:5345; scurrilious, i.e. calumnious (against men), or (specially) impious (against God):
KJV - blasphemer (-mous), railing.

NT:5345
NT:5345 pheme (fay'-may); from NT:5346; a saying, i.e. rumor ("fame"):
KJV - fame.

I saw that the word quench meant to EXTINGUISH. It is saying, "Do not extinguish or let the flame of the Holy Spirit go out!" At that moment the Holy Spirit flooded the following scriptures into my heart. I saw that it was possible to have the light of the Holy Spirit go out in churches and denominations:

Rev 2:4-6 NKJV
Nevertheless I have this against you, that you have left your first love. Remember therefore from where you have fallen; repent and do the first works, or else I will come to you quickly and remove your lampstand from its place — unless you repent.

And I saw that it was possible to have the light of the Holy Spirit be extinguished in our own lives:

Matt 25:5-13 NKJV
But while the bridegroom was delayed, they all slumbered and slept. "And at midnight a cry was heard: 'Behold, the bridegroom is coming; go out to meet him!' 7 Then all those

virgins arose and trimmed their lamps . And the foolish said to the wise, 'Give us some of your oil, for our lamps are going out.' But the wise answered, saying, 'No, lest there should not be enough for us and you; but go rather to those who sell, and buy for yourselves.' And while they went to buy, the bridegroom came, and those who were ready went in with him to the wedding; and the door was shut. "Afterward the other virgins came also, saying, 'Lord, Lord, open to us!' But he answered and said, 'Assuredly, I say to you, I do not know you.' "Watch therefore, for you know neither the day nor the hour in which the Son of Man is coming.

ENLIGHTENMENT COMES: I realized with total clarity that because the Holy Spirit had been quenched, all these churches and denominations that once knew the Holy Spirit were taken into famine and then finally their lights went out and they were given over to demons.

I saw the culmination of the many prophets and sent ones who were rejected and stoned and spilled their blood to be able to defend the Holy Spirit and declare His Word. Outside of a small remnant that He has preserved, I understood that each and every door He has knocked on in history has put Him in a smaller and smaller place... to the point that entire families, churches, denominations, cities, and countries had been under the curse of famine for hearing Him.

Amos 8:7-13 NKJV
The LORD has sworn by the pride of Jacob: "Surely I will never forget any of their works. 8 Shall the land not tremble for this, And everyone mourn who dwells in it? All of it shall swell like the River, Heave and subside Like the River of Egypt. 9 "And it shall come to pass in that day," says the Lord GOD, "That I will make the sun go down at noon, And I will darken the earth in broad daylight; 10 I will turn your feasts into mourning, And all your songs into lamentation; I will bring sackcloth on every waist, And baldness on every head; I will make it like mourning for an only son, And its end like a bitter day. 11 "Behold, the days are coming," says the

Lord GOD, "That I will send a famine on the land, Not a famine of bread, Nor a thirst for water, But of hearing the words of the LORD. 12 They shall wander from sea to sea, And from north to east; They shall run to and fro, seeking the word of the LORD, But shall not find it. 13 "In that day the fair virgins And strong young men Shall faint from thirst.

I could not stop sobbing. My heart was breaking for Him, for His people and for the plight of the earth today. We are an endtime generation, the culmination product in bearing the harvest of all the decisions to resist the Holy Spirit. I asked the Lord to forgive us for grieving His Holy Spirit. I asked Him to please forgive us for quenching Him and putting Him in such a small, hindered place in our lives, families and churches. I asked Him to forgive us for despising His Words through the prophets, and for killing all those He sent to us as His warnings, pleadings, and knockings. I asked that He would, in His mercy, give us a second chance and break the curse over the world's ears to hear His voice. I asked that He would come once again and rain upon us and that He would give us grace to receive Him in His fullest expression.

THE FAMINE FOR HEARING GOD:
I have had several visions of the baldheaded principality over the famine for hearing God. I have repeatedly asked the Lord how to break the famine over the ears of His people, when we are crying out for intimacy to hear Him and know Him deeper than ever before. He has taken me through many layers of understanding and repentance on how we have grieved Him by how we treat others, by the stoniness of our own hearts, by dabbling in sin, unforgiveness, controlling the Holy Spirit in meetings, using soul power to replace His power, meddling in pride and blindness, and compromising and ignoring scripture.

But this time, the Lord brought back the phrase, "Hell hath no fury like a women scorned." It was one of the phrases I had heard in one of the visions where I was pursuing this ruler over famine of hearing God. I understood the passion

211

of God, to have long suffered all these years in pursuit of love. And then the next revelation hit me.

THE FEAR OF GOD:
I have often heard (and experienced this myself) that the depths of someone's anger and/or rage is the opposite of their depth of need to be loved, or having experienced loved then lost it. I saw the opposite side of His fury in that same light of Him experiencing such long suffering of being so constrained throughout all history.

All these years the Holy Spirit has visited. He knocks and we answer the door and He comes in. He stays as long as we welcome Him in that place and then He falls back and leaves that place of intimacy and abides in the other doors of our heart that we give Him access. It has been a constant request and invitation process of coming and going wherever He is welcomed in our lives. But we have not yet experienced His habitation.

Jesus spoke of this as abiding in Him, the Vine. Instead, we jump off the vine until we make a mess and then we cling back on the vine until we are fixed up again. We know so little of what it really means to dwell with Him in habitation, where our lives are no longer our own, but we are one with Him.

When the Holy Spirit comes as a habitation, there will be very little room for quenching Him. It will no longer be a constant request and invitation of moving from room to room, and either finding more or less of us for fellowship. Rather, it will be a marriage of oneness that can not be separated. And if we pull back from Him in a place where we were yoked and bonded as one with Him, it would be the same as divorce. In such a place, if the Holy Spirit is despised it will provoke the Father's fury.

I believe I understand this like never before. I feel like I have had a glimpse into the days of Ananias and Sapphira, who lost their lives because they dared to lie in the Holy

Presence of the Holy Spirit. Next time the Holy Spirit rains on His people, and all flesh, there will be a much more serious price to pay than just dull ears and hearts in a famine of hearing Him. Just like the days of Ananias and Sapphira, there will be a much more serious a price to pay for despising Him and not treating Him with respect, because next time He is coming for a habitation, not a visitation.

Acts 5:9-11 NKJV
Then Peter said to her, "How is it that you have agreed together to test the Spirit of the Lord? Look, the feet of those who have buried your husband are at the door, and they will carry you out." 10 Then immediately she fell down at his feet and breathed her last. And the young men came in and found her dead, and carrying her out, buried her by her husband. 11 So great fear came upon all the church and upon all who heard these things.

Heb 6:4-6 NKJV
For it is impossible for those who were once enlightened , and have tasted the heavenly gift, and have become partakers of the Holy Spirit, and have tasted the good word of God and the powers of the age to come, if they fall away, to renew them again to repentance, since they crucify again for themselves the Son of God, and put Him to an open shame.

WORD TO PONDER: YOU COMFORT ME WHEN YOU LISTEN 1/27/08
My friends, you have not understood how deeply you comfort Me when you give Me your time and listen to My Word. It soothes My heart to search the whole world and find the candles in your window shining so brightly! You are up and waiting for My knock. You are asking and hopeful; always requesting more of Me. To find such friends is very rare, and I just want to thank you for being My friend.

As you have opened more and more of your heart-doors to Me, I have come in and we have supped together in ever deepening levels. Such a joy it has been to commune and sup together as you listen, ponder, pray and share. It means so much that you want to know what I think and feel and understand My ways. It means so much that you have given Me room. It means so much that you are willing to lay down your life so that I can have more expression on earth. Thank you beloved friends.

Rev 3:20 NKJV
Behold, I stand at the door and knock . If anyone hears My voice and opens the door, I will come in to him and dine with him, and he with Me.

PRAYER ON OCTOBER 31

We unite together and pray as one,
As we stand on behalf of Your kingdom.
Forgive us our sins when we are led astray.
Our flesh is corrupt, it keeps us from Your ways.

As the enemies gather to curse our land,
We gather in faith in Your power to stand.
It's not in ourselves to hold up a shield,
Or in our own might with our swords to wield.

The blood of Jesus is our great power to fight.
It covers our backs that no curses will alight.
We humble ourselves, thanking You for Jesus' blood.
His blood lifts us up, above all demonic flood.

By Your Spirit we connect in Your true love.
Your banner is spread out in heaven above,
Reigning Supremely over demonic hordes.
We gather together and call You Lord.

We pray for our loved ones both near and far
To cover their backsides from the bizarre.

214

We ask You replace that power to curse
With blessings upon us, to reimburse.

We lay in ruins among our decay,
In the stolen years of pain and delay.
Instead rebuild us through our prayers and love.
Please send us Your Spirit, Your sweet, sweet Dove.

Jesus' blood puts all devils under foot.
As we command, "Back off, we want our loot."
We rest in Jesus as we rise in faith.
We burst forth in freedom above the scathe.

Let this year be mighty in the power of Your blood
As You reveal Aaron's rod, the one that has bud.
Drenched in Your Presence before Your great ark
Now releasing Your power among the dark.

Go forth oh rod to protect and defend.
Demarcate the line among every man.
Cover the righteous with mercy and declare
The Justice of God among men everywhere.

It is time to level the playing field,
To balance the scales from what was yield
From the crops of men not given reward.
Now bow the knee that Jesus Christ is Lord.

Ps 110:1-4 NKJV
*The LORD said to my Lord, "Sit at My right hand, Till I make
Your enemies Your footstool." The LORD shall send the rod of
Your strength out of Zion. Rule in the midst of Your enemies!
Your people shall be volunteers In the day of Your power; In the
beauties of holiness, from the womb of the morning, You have the
dew of Your youth. The LORD has sworn And will not relent, "You
are a priest forever According to the order of Melchizedek."*

PRAYER ON SUNDOWN YOM KIPPER

This is the night where the line is drawn.
Separating the year of rights and wrong.
Their hearts and deeds went through the maze.
My sheep pass before Me now as I gaze.

Exposed, uncovered and cameras on them.
Walking before Me having pulled up their hems.
Now they pass under My rod.
I look at their feet, are they well shod?

The foundations of their walk are inspected so close.
Arches strengthened, clean between toes?
Ankles turned in, ankles turned out?
Level and secure, holy devout?

I see their feet and how they walk,
I check their pace and match their talk.
This year what matters is to be shod with peace.
There's only one way to walk in My grace:

Repentance, confession, humility.
Apologize quick for tranquility.
Mend your fences, and secure your doors.
Walk a straight path on hardwood floors.

Don't let the enemy steal your peace.
Keep your shoes on and keep them laced.
Receive correction if you need new shoes.
Hold onto what works, or you will lose.

I speak through men, but listen to Me.
And you will walk into your destiny.
Men will nurture and men will teach.
Men will betray and men will breach.

Hold onto the good and release the bad.
Keep your focus on Me, not the sad.
Some are ready and some are not.
Another year's wait for what's been sought.

Those who are shod with peace in their walk.
Are ready to move and ready to talk.
Move on to the right and walk on through.
Hearing My Word and then promptly DO.

I will set up your places with divine appointments.
Tabernacle's covering you just like a tent.
Hidden and secure and warm inside.
I surround My sent ones and walk by their side.

Prov 4:10-15 NKJV
Hear, my son, and receive my sayings, and the years of your life
will be many. I have taught you in the way of wisdom; I have led
you in right paths. When you walk , your steps will not be
hindered, and when you run, you will not stumble. Take firm hold
of instruction, do not let go; Keep her, for she is your life. Do not
enter the path of the wicked, and do not walk in the way of evil.
Avoid it, do not travel on it; Turn away from it and pass on.

THE QUICKENED WORD WEBSITE MINISTRY

www.thequickenedword.com

~ THE QUICKENED WORD ~
Quickened Words for Hungry & Searching Hearts

The Quickened Word shares timely prophetic insights through a variety of means: Visions · Dreams · Still Small Voice · Words to Ponder · Articles · Scriptural Studies · Quickened Quotes · Quickened Stories · Parables · Ears2Hear

In 1984 Sandy Warner had a personal visitation from Jesus Christ in which He handed her a solid gold pen. He planted within her an anointing and passion to encourage a hurting world and to teach others how to hear the Lord.

Sandy releases to her readers only what the Holy Spirit has quickened to her as prophetic, personal, timely, applicable and helpful.

John 6:63
It is the spirit that quickeneth; the flesh profiteth nothing: the words that I speak unto you, they are spirit, and they are life.

E-MAIL LIST: Sent to Equip & Encourage

Subscribe by sending an email to:
thequickenedword-subscribe@MyInJesus.com

BOOKS
Soft Cover * Hard Cover * E-Books

1]   101+ Ways God Speaks (And How To Hear Him)
2]   The Baptism of the Holy Spirit
3]   The Journey of Our Faith – More Precious Than Gold
4]   Discernment: Separating the Holy From the Profane
5]   Your Authority in Christ Jesus
6]   Ministering Deliverance
7]   Intercessors Arise & Finding Your Authority
8]   God Speaks Through Humor and Bloopers
9]   Lessons in Warfare
10]   Beautiful Butterfly: God's Mystery
11]   Angels and Demons
12]   In Synch: God's Call to Unity
13]   Parables & Signs: God's Hidden Love Stories
14]   A Way Out of the Maze
15]   Words to Ponder
16]   All Aboard the Glory Train
17]   The School of Ears2Hear
18]   Gold Fever
19]   Poetry to Ponder
20]   Rain & Glory
21]   Spanish: 101+ Ways God Speaks (And How To Hear Him)
22]   QW Articles
23]   Annie's Visions - Books 1 - 4 combined
24]   Moments of Intimacy – Grandma Anna's Selahs
25]   Climbing Higher – Grandma Anna's Selahs Volume 2
26]   Walk With Me

LaVergne, TN USA
26 July 2010
190917LV00003B/81/P